The Almost Healthy Cookbook

Fine Food for a
Modern Lifestyle

Ann Creber

GREENHOUSE
PUBLICATIONS

First published in 1988 by
Greenhouse Publications Pty Ltd
122–126 Ormond Road
Elwood 3184 Victoria Australia

© Ann Creber 1988

Cover design by Sharon Carr
Book design by Leonie Stott
Photography by Phil Wymant
Illustrations by Jenny Darling
Typeset in Bembo by Meredith Typesetters, Melbourne
Printed in Australia by Impact Printing (Victoria) Pty Ltd

National Library of Australia
Cataloguing-in-publication data:

Creber, Ann, 1930–
    The almost healthy cookbook.

    Includes index.
    ISBN 0 86436 168 8.

    1. Cookery. I. Title.
641.5

Cover photograph: Lazy Days Luncheon

ACKNOWLEDGEMENTS

Any cookbook needs input from a number of people, and this one is no exception. Firstly, my thanks to Greenhouse Publications for encouraging me to undertake this project; particular thanks to Marg Bowman, good friend and sympathetic editor. I am also indebted to Leonie Stott, whose tasteful design has considerably enhanced the book.

Warm thanks too to Cathie Graham, daughter and associate, who looked after the logistics and ensured that the recipes were accurately typed and eventually reached the publisher more or less on time!

I am grateful to my assistant, Leonie (Ashworth) Clarke and to Janet Lodge, who assisted in recipe testing and in preparing food for photography.

Phil Wymant, long-time associate and patient friend, contributed his talent and creativity to produce the photographs in this book. Michael Patton assisted him and also played a major part in helping with props.

Most of the props were provided by Eve Munday, 8 River Street, South Yarra, and I am very grateful for the generosity of this company.

Finally, as always, warm thanks to the shop proprietors and staff who allow me to select beautiful food for photography.

Ann Creber

For Holly — with love

CONTENTS

INTRODUCTION

I suppose I must admit that with this book I am making a statement about my own attitude towards food and its place in our lives.

As a child, I was influenced by a grandmother (a slim grandmother!) who loved food – loved to grow, gather, cook and serve food. And for me, many of my happiest childhood memories are of misty autumn mornings when Nanna and I tramped over the paddocks seeking mushrooms, and of warm autumn afternoons when we diligently gathered windfall apples from local orchards and spotty quinces from gnarled old trees growing along creek banks.

Summer was made memorable by the desperate need to gather the always too-rapidly ripening plums and tomatoes and to convert them into the savoury chutneys and sweet jams we enjoyed all winter. Another summer memory is of stripping dried herbs from their twigs and of the warm fragrance of honey straight from Nanna's bee hives.

You see, my early association with food was a happy one and it disturbs me that so often now there is a sense of guilt and anxiety which pervades our approach towards eating. Over a number of years when I worked in weight control, I became acutely aware of this and always endeavoured to eliminate the feeling of guilt in the dieters with whom I worked. I felt this to be an essential element in any successful weight control programme; I still do.

This guilty attitude seems to destroy for many people the pleasure of eating, which is a perfectly natural and desirable one. Certainly there are many instances where it is essential, or at least desirable, that specific foods be avoided by certain people and many excellent books have been published to meet these needs.

However, I believe that for most of us the sensible and happy solution is found in following an eating programme which emphasises 'moderation'. Most of my friends eat the kind of food this book offers. They are well aware of the important health factors to be considered, but they are also, for social or professional reasons, almost obliged to eat at least some of those foods which are frequently – and I think sometimes unfairly – labelled nowadays as 'unhealthy'.

In this category I would include dairy products, oil, red meats and wine. I firmly believe that for the average healthy person moderate amounts of all these foods may be safely and sensibly included in the diet. And much can be achieved by compromise. For those like myself who love butter, there is the healthier alternative of a dairy spread consisting of 70 per cent butter and 30 per cent polyunsaturated oil. The flavour is that of butter, but the cholesterol level is considerably lowered. Likewise with milk. I loathe skim milk, but find the fat-reduced version perfectly acceptable and healthier.

Olive oil, once carefully avoided by many health purists, is now generally recognised as having positive health benefits, and I use it in preference to most other oils. Again, it is desirable to reduce the quantity used to the lowest acceptable levels, and you will find that in many recipe books you can reduce the quantity dramatically with excellent results. Experiment with the new extra-light olive oils on the market and learn to appreciate their delicate fruitiness.

Sugar content can be reduced in most standard recipes, and, where it is an essential ingredient in some dishes, experiment until you find the lowest acceptable quantity you can use to achieve satisfactory results.

You will find that in most of my recipes in this book, salt is almost entirely excluded. I use a negligible amount myself these days (still can't face a boiled egg without a tiny sprinkle!) and am trying to eliminate it entirely. Be generous in your use of herbs and spices and you will find that their flavours do make salt unnecessary.

The menus in this book have been balanced to avoid an excess of fat, sugar, etc. in any one meal. For example, if there is a pastry in the main course, the entree and dessert will be light and with little or no shortening used, or, if it is, as an optional ingredient.

For those who are reluctant to use eggs, for example, remember that if a recipe for six uses two eggs there is a very small amount of egg per person. Likewise, if a tablespoon of liqueur is used in a dish for four, one teaspoonful per person is not too damaging. There is an emphasis on high fibre foods, and my own preference is for wholegrain foods wherever possible. Vegetables are used extensively and fruits feature prominently in many desserts.

Salads play an important part in my own culinary life – I feel desperately deprived if I can't have a salad every day. To ensure freshness and variety, cultivate your own little patch of lettuce and other greens and grow your own herbs for their flavour and fragrance. (Their flowers look great, too, as a garnish!)

I have a plot in our local community garden, which enables me to experiment with a whole range of exotic greens – and to get a bit of exercise at the end of a spade! Most of the meat dishes in this book tend towards the use of white meats, especially chicken, rather than red meat. I must admit this is partly because of personal preference; I like the delicacy of its flavour. However, unless you are prepared to take the time and trouble to carefully strip all skin and fat from the chicken, there is not much benefit in choosing it in preference to red meat. Moderate amounts of red meats, from free-range cattle and with every particle of fat removed, is still a good and acceptable ingredient for most people. (A well grilled little chop is one of the culinary delights of the world!)

Fish, too, is an excellent choice provided it is cooked appropriately. Avoid deep frying and the use of batter, except on rare and indulgent occasions, and settle for poaching, baking or grilling. Do be sure you choose the right fish for the cooking method you prefer; for example, a dry-fleshed fish does not grill successfully.

Alcohol is always a contentious issue in relation to healthy eating. A couple of glasses of dry wine seems to be an acceptable amount for most people and it does complement good food. I don't drink any spirits or fortified wines and generally use

3

them in cooking only when their alcohol content is removed by boiling.

Many of the dishes in these menus may be juggled, of course, to provide a wider range of menus of your own choosing. (Just keep an eye on the balance and ensure that there is not an excessive use of any of the less 'healthy' ingredients.) Using these, it is possible to entertain without guests being aware that they are really eating 'almost healthily'!

It is vital to remember that the size of the serving is important. My own appetite is not huge, so some cooks may find these portions rather light – and that is another area of compromise, of course. Balancing meals through the day is also essential in our 'almost healthy' eating programme. If one eats a hearty lunch, then a very light dinner is most desirable. I think, too, that one should avoid drinking alcohol with both lunch and dinner; soda water with a dash of bitters is a good choice for a pre-meal aperitif.

I know there will be many health purists who will strongly disagree both with the philosophy I follow and the recipes I offer. I emphasise that this book is **not** for the purists. It is for the people like me who love to eat, who love to cook and who really enjoy sharing the pleasures of the table with their 'almost healthy' friends.

Good health and bon appetit!

Ann Creber

Note: Where an asterisk appears after a dish or serving suggestion in the menus, no recipe has been supplied.

A TASTE OF SUMMER

This menu takes advantage of the flavours of summer. Pears, summer vegetables and herbs, and the luscious stone fruits which are with us all too fleetingly, feature in these dishes. Take time off one summer day to enjoy them ...

The Medley of Summer Garden Delights is particularly marvellous if you are a gardener or have access to the freshest little vegetables, but, even if you have to rely on those from shop or market, it is still one of the most enjoyable of all dishes.

For those concerned with extra kilojoules, the shredded crêpe, although an interesting addition to the flambéed fruits, may be sacrificed in the interests of the waistline.

CREAM OF PEAR AND CELERY SOUP

GARLIC AND LEMON MARINATED
CHICKEN KEBABS

MEDLEY OF SUMMER GARDEN DELIGHTS

PECAN STUDDED RYE BREAD

FLAMBEED FRUITS WITH SHREDDED
CREPES

CREAM OF PEAR AND CELERY SOUP

Serves 6–8

Don't be deterred by this unlikely combination
of ingredients – it really is a delightful soup.
I prefer it cold, but others seem to enjoy it as
a hot dish.

1 tbsp butter
4 white onions, chopped
1 bunch celery, finely chopped
6 cups chicken stock
375–500g ripe pears, peeled, cored and finely sliced
½ cup unflavoured yoghurt
freshly ground white pepper to taste
few drops Tabasco
celery leaves and pear slices as a garnish

Melt butter in a large, heavy saucepan over low heat. Add
onions, cover and cook until translucent, stirring occasionally,
about 10 minutes. Add chopped celery, cover and cook until
softened, stirring occasionally, about 10 minutes. Add stock
and bring to the boil. Reduce heat and simmer until celery is
tender. Add pears and simmer until tender. Place in blender or
food processor and purée until smooth. Add yoghurt and
blend in.

Season with pepper, and add a couple of drops of Tabasco to
each bowl before serving. This soup may be served hot or
cold, garnished with wafer thin pear slices and celery leaves.

GARLIC AND LEMON MARINATED CHICKEN KEBABS

Serves 6

This tangy recipe is one I love and often serve as part of a buffet, either hot or cold. Cut chicken breasts into strips to transform them to finger food, or use chicken wings for a cheap and easy alternative.

750g chicken thigh meat or breast fillets, all skin
  removed
⅓ cup extra-light olive oil
juice of 2 lemons
2 cloves garlic, finely chopped
ground pepper
bay leaves, preferably small, fresh ones

Cut meat into cubes. Combine oil, lemon juice, garlic and pepper and mix well. Place chicken meat into a shallow bowl, pour on the marinade and allow to stand for up to 24 hours. Turn the meat often.

To cook, thread the chicken meat onto soaked satay sticks, alternating with pieces of bay leaf. Brush well with the marinade and cook under hot, preheated griller. Allow about 5 minutes each side, turning as necessary and brushing with any remaining marinade. Serve at once.

Note: The pieces of bay leaf will char – this doesn't worry me. I see it as part of the 'reality' of food, but if it concerns you, leave the bay leaves off the satays and just add a couple of them to the marinade.

A MEDLEY OF SUMMER GARDEN DELIGHTS

Serves 6

For me, this is the supreme summer meal for 'the evening after the night before', when I have eaten a large, rich meal as a guest or at a restaurant. It is also a good choice for an evening meal after one has eaten lunch as a main meal. The success of this dish depends on cooking the vegetables in the correct sequence, and to avoid over cooking.

500g small green beans, topped and tailed
12 baby carrots, scrubbed and halved lengthwise
6 very small parsnips, peeled and halved lengthwise
12 baby button squash, halved
185g small snow peas or sugar peas, topped and tailed
⅓ cup very finely chopped parsley or 1 tbsp very finely
*   chopped mixed herbs (such as basil, marjoram,*
*   thyme, rosemary etc.)*
3 tbsp butter or butter/oil blend
plenty of freshly ground pepper

Bring a large saucepan of water to the boil. (I use a pasta cooker which has a full depth, removable strainer insert. If you prefer, use a steamer.) Add the beans and cook for about 6 minutes, then add carrots and cook for a further 3 minutes. Add parsnips and cook for 3 minutes. Add squash, cook for 3 minutes, then the peas and cook another 3 minutes. (According to my barely adequate arithmetic, this allows about 18 minutes in all.)

Drain quickly, then place vegetables, parsley and herbs, butter and pepper in the pot or a large bowl and serve at once.

I like to serve the vegetables in a large, preheated, fairly deep platter and allow guests to help themselves.

Scrubbed baby carmine potatoes are delicious in this combination, too. If you use these, they need to be started about 5 minutes before the beans are added.

I love to serve little asparagus spears as well, and usually give them about 8 minutes. If you prefer, vegetables may be julienned – this does not change the cooking sequence but does shorten actual cooking time. The main thing to remember is that each vegetable must still retain its crispness and colour.

PECAN STUDDED RYE BREAD

Makes 1 loaf

15g compressed yeast
1 tsp honey
500ml lukewarm water
250g white flour
250g rye flour
1 tsp salt (optional)
60g pecan nuts, very coarsely chopped

Crumble compressed yeast into a small bowl, then add honey and a little water. Blend together with a spoon. Add the remainder of the water. Stand bowl in a warm place until liquid froths.

Mix flours, salt and nuts together in a large bowl. Make a well in the centre and pour in the frothing liquid. Stir with a wooden spoon until mixed and then knead dough until it is of a smooth, manageable consistency. Shape into a ball, return to basin, cover and allow to stand in a warm place until dough doubles in size.

Punch down, then shape into a loaf and place in a small, greased bread tin. Allow to stand until dough rises to the top of the tin; brush with egg yolk mixed with a little water. Place into a preheated 200°C oven and bake for 10 minutes; reduce heat to 190°C and cook for a further 40 minutes.

When cooked, remove from tin and cool on a wire rack.

Serve thinly sliced with soups or entrées or on a cheese board.

FLAMBEED FRUITS WITH SHREDDED CREPES

Serves 6

CREPES

¼ cup plain flour
1 egg
⅓ cup milk

FRUIT FLAMBE

45g dairy spread or margarine
⅓ cup honey
1 cup orange juice
good squeeze of lemon juice
1 tbsp brandy (optional)
1 tbsp Grand Marnier (optional)
250g fresh apricots or plums
4 medium peaches
4 bananas
1 punnet strawberries

To make crêpes, sift flour into bowl, add egg and stir until mixture is free of lumps. Gradually add milk, and stir until smooth. Place a small piece of butter into hot pancake pan and swirl around pan. Pour about 2 tablespoons of mixture into pan, swirl around and cook until golden brown underneath; toss or turn and brown other side. Stack crêpes as they cook and keep warm.

For fruit flambé, heat butter in a large pan, add honey, orange juice and lemon juice and stir until simmering. Add brandy and Grand Marnier, heat and set aflame. When flames die down, simmer uncovered for 2 minutes.

Place halved apricots into pan, spooning sauce over them, then halved and skinned peaches. Push the fruit to one side of pan and add peeled and thickly sliced bananas and strawberries. Keep each fruit separate. Simmer uncovered for 4 minutes, spooning sauce over fruit frequently.

Roll crêpes and cut into shreds. Mix with the fruits and pour over sauce. Garnish with sugared mint leaves (see recipe p 66).

'A GOOD BREAKFAST'

When I was a child, 'a good breakfast' would have included such hearty items as eggs and bacon or scrambled eggs or grilled sausages and tomatoes. Our attitudes – and appetites – have changed, and most people find now that a light breakfast is sufficient to meet their needs.

With the new awareness of the importance of a high fibre diet, muesli has of course become a commonplace breakfast dish and there are many excellent varieties available on the market. However, in case you wish to make up your own, I include a tasty version. Fruits and juices have found a regular place on the breakfast table, of course, and I suggest that you use a selection of tropical fruits in this menu. I discovered the joy of freshly squeezed lime juice on exotic fruits when I was in Thailand, and breakfasted on that the whole time I was there.

Lemon juice is less exotic, but provides the same tang.

HOMEMADE MUESLI WITH YOGHURT

LIBERTY HOUSE BLUEBERRY MUFFINS

TROPICAL FRUITS WITH LIME JUICE*

HERBAL TEA, REGULAR TEA OR COFFEE*

HOMEMADE MUESLI

2 cups rolled oats
1 cup rolled rye
1 cup processed bran (or natural bran, if preferred)
½ cup lightly toasted sesame seeds
½ cup toasted sunflower seeds
½ cup coarsely chopped dried apricots
½ cup coarsely chopped dried figs
½ cup pitted and chopped prunes
½ cup sultanas or raisins
½ cup shredded coconut
½ cup chopped nuts
½ cup lecithin meal (optional)

Combine all ingredients in a **very** large bowl and mix well. Store in a tightly covered container. You might like to follow my Nanna's advice and add a couple of bay leaves to the container in which you keep it. She swore this kept away weevils, and I have to say that it has always worked for me...

LIBERTY HOUSE BLUEBERRY MUFFINS

Makes 12

One of my favourite retreats is an old-fashioned guest house at Hepburn Springs. 'Liberty House' is within walking distance of the spas and the bath-houses and it is wonderfully restorative to spend a weekend there.

An added incentive is the delicious blueberry muffins served for breakfast – and at any other time that the urge arises – by Cate McKinnon. I begged this recipe from her, and share it now with you. They are so good that served warm they need no butter.

1 banana, mashed
¼ cup vegetable oil
⅓ cup honey
¾ cup milk
1 cup wholemeal self raising flour
1 cup white self raising flour
¾ cup fresh or canned blueberries, very well drained

Mix together banana, oil, honey and milk. Add the flours and mix very lightly – remember that muffin batter should be only just mixed. Stir in the blueberries.

Spoon into 12 lightly greased muffin pans. Bake in a preheated moderate oven for about 20 minutes. Serve warm.

These do freeze well, so it is worth making up a reasonably large quantity and tucking them into the freezer for future breakfasts.

A DO-AHEAD MEAL FOR SIX

This menu could be served as a late-night meal after a film or the theatre, as a casual luncheon or as an evening meal. When the dairy food and fats are divided into six portions, their content is quite low and the obviously healthy elements in this menu balance them out.

These little pancakes are most versatile and provide an excellent base for vegetarian fillings. I sometimes combine cooked chopped pumpkin, creamed corn, chopped spring onion and parsley for a delicious alternative.

SALMON AND AVOCADO PATE IN
TOMATO CASES

CUMIN PARSLEY CREPES WITH CHICKEN
AND CAPSICUM FILLING

CELERIAC WITH LEMON MAYONNAISE

FIGS POACHED IN RED WINE WITH
ORANGE SEGMENTS

SALMON AND AVOCADO PATE IN TOMATO CASES

Serves 6

1 medium avocado
1 × 220g can pink or red salmon, drained and flaked
1 tbsp yoghurt or sour cream
pepper
juice of 1 lemon
3 or 4 sprigs of parsley, roughly chopped
½ clove garlic, crushed or finely chopped
grated peel of ½ lemon
6 well shaped medium tomatoes, scooped out

Scoop out all flesh from the avocado; combine with salmon and all other ingredients, except tomatoes. Place into blender or food processor and blend until very smooth. If preferred, a hand mouli may be used; in this case, parsley should be finely chopped and added afterwards.

Spoon pâté into hollowed out tomatoes and chill.

Serve with triangles of fresh wholemeal bread and butter or toast.

CUMIN PARSLEY CREPES

Makes about 16

1 cup plain flour
1 cup skim milk
3 large eggs
2 tbsp butter, melted and cooled
2 tsp ground cumin
3 tbsp very finely chopped parsley
extra-light olive oil for frying

In a food processor bowl combine the flour, skim milk, eggs, cooled butter and cumin. Process until blended, scrape sides of bowl with spatula and blend for a further 20 seconds. Transfer to a bowl and stir in finely chopped parsley.

Heat a crêpe pan or non-stick pan (about 15–18 cm) and brush with oil. Heat until moderately hot, then spoon in about 1½–2 tablespoons of the mixture, tilting pan to spread evenly over base. Return pan to heat and cook crêpe until brown on underside. Turn over and lightly brown second side. Continue brushing pan and preparing crêpes in the same way until all the mixture is used.

They may be stacked, wrapped in plastic film and refrigerated for up to 3 days – they also freeze quite well. (If making up in advance, fill and roll pancakes at serving time. Place into a shallow dish and reheat gently in a moderate oven. They may be loosely covered with a piece of foil.)

CHICKEN AND CAPSICUM FILLING

Serves 8

1 cup cold cooked chicken or turkey, diced
pepper to taste
2 tsp lemon juice
¼ cup red and yellow capsicum, chopped or julienned
¼ cup light sour cream or unflavoured yoghurt
chopped parsley

Season chicken with pepper and lemon juice and marinate 30 minutes. Combine with capsicum and sour cream or yoghurt. Heat gently in a small saucepan.

Place small amount in centre of crêpe and roll.

CELERIAC WITH LEMON MAYONNAISE

Serves 6

Few people take advantage of the interesting flavour and texture of the knobbly celeriac root. It makes a good vegetable steamed or boiled and in this salad provides an interesting flavour and plenty of crunch.

As only a portion of the mayonnaise is used, store the remainder in the refrigerator for future use. It will last for up to a week.

1 large celeriac root, peeled
1 tbsp prepared horseradish
pepper

LEMON MAYONNAISE

1 cup extra-light olive oil
2 egg yolks
2 tbsp lemon juice
1 tsp dry mustard
little salt (optional)
good pinch cayenne pepper
2 tbsp coarsely chopped fresh dill

Grate celeriac and mix with horseradish and pepper. Using one-third of the lemon mayonnaise, toss together celeriac mixture. (If celeriac is prepared in advance, place into acidulated water to prevent browning. Drain well and pat dry before using.)

To make mayonnaise, pour ¼ cup oil into blender and add egg yolks, lemon juice, sugar, mustard, salt and cayenne. Blend for 10 seconds. Add remaining oil in a fine stream with the motor running. When all the oil has been added, add the dill and blend in. If mayonnaise is to be kept for some days, stir in 1 tablespoon of boiling water.

Keep covered under refrigeration.

FIGS POACHED IN RED WINE WITH ORANGE SEGMENTS

Serves 6

2 cups dry red wine
¼ cup raw sugar
½ kg plump dried figs
½ tbsp orange liqueur (optional)
4 navel oranges, peeled and pith removed
julienned orange peel for garnish

In a saucepan, combine the wine and sugar, bring to the boil and simmer. Stir until the sugar is dissolved. Add figs and simmer until tender, then add orange liqueur. Using a slotted spoon, transfer figs to a bowl and boil liquid until it becomes syrupy. Pour syrup over figs and allow to cool to room temperature.

Place in the centre of a serving platter. Cut the oranges into segments between membranes and arrange the segments around the figs.

Garnish with julienned orange peel and a sprig of mint or a tiny edible blossom.

Opposite: A Taste of Summer, see page 5
Overleaf: 'A Good Breakfast', see page 11

LAZY DAYS LUNCHEON

The luscious ingredients for this menu are with us in the late summer, and I enjoyed this easy meal with friends on a warm Sunday recently. There is almost no advance preparation at all – unless you plan to make your own pasta – and it really does offer 'almost healthy' eating without appearing to do so.

FRESH FIG AND WATERCRESS SALAD

PASTA WITH WALNUTS, CREAM AND TOMATO

SALAD OF CELERY, FENNEL AND CUCUMBER

CANTALOUPE WITH PORT

Opposite: Lazy Days Luncheon, see page 19
Overleaf: A Do-Ahead Meal for Six, see page 14

FRESH FIG AND WATERCRESS SALAD

Serves 4

This tangy dressing complements the lushness of the sun-ripened figs, and the contrasting textures and flavours make this an interesting side salad or a light first course. As this salad requires only a small amount of dressing, cover and chill the remainder.

2 tbsp raspberry vinegar
1 tbsp French mustard
1 tsp finely grated fresh ginger root
freshly ground pepper
½ cup light olive oil
1 bunch watercress or two cups mesculn*
4 lusciously ripe figs, stem trimmed and flesh 'fanned'

Pour vinegar into a small bowl, then add mustard, ginger and pepper, and stir. Very gradually add the olive oil, whisking all the time.

Wash cress or mesculn and shake or pat until quite dry. Toss with a little dressing.

Place greens onto 4 small serving plates, top with fan-sliced figs and serve at once.

*Mesculn is a mixture of various salad greens picked and sold while they are still tiny. Better fruiterers often carry this now. An alternative is to plant masses of salad greens yourself and prune them as you require them!

PASTA WITH WALNUTS, CREAM AND TOMATO

Serves 4

⅔ cup light cream*
½ cup tomatoes, chopped
¼ cup white wine
3 tbsp finely chopped black olives
3 tbsp chopped fresh parsley
2 tsp lemon juice
375g fettuccine, freshly cooked
1 tbsp olive oil (optional)
125g prosciutto or lean ham, cut into julienne strips
¼ cup chopped toasted walnuts
freshly grated Parmesan cheese

Combine cream, tomatoes, wine, olives, parsley and lemon juice in a medium saucepan and simmer until sauce thickens slightly, about 10 minutes, stirring occasionally.

Place pasta in bowl, add oil (if using) and toss well. Pour sauce over pasta and top with prosciutto and walnuts (and do toast them – the difference in flavour makes it worth the effort.) Sprinkle with Parmesan.

*Use half milk/half cream or half cream/half chicken stock if preferred.

SALAD OF CELERY, FENNEL AND CUCUMBER

Serves 4

Crunchy, with a combination of interesting flavours, this salad goes well with a wide range of other foods. Serve it with any of the dressings or mayonnaises suggested in this book, but for this version I feel a simple French dressing would be best.

heart of a small bunch of celery, sliced
1 small fennel bulb
1 small unpeeled Continental cucumber, thinly sliced

Prepare celery. Remove all coarse outer leaves of the fennel and discard. Cut remaining portion into very thin slices and add to the celery.

Combine the finely sliced cucumber with other ingredients. Toss together, add a little pepper if desired, and sprinkle on a little French dressing.

CANTALOUPE WITH PORT

Serves 4

Even if one had never experienced the delights of eating lush ripe cantaloupe, who could resist this description by Colette, that wonderful French writer – 'a cantaloupe, mysterious as a well, which has drunk a whole glass of port and two teaspoons of sugar'.

I offer my version of this simple but voluptuous dessert.

1 small cantaloupe (rockmelon)
2 tbsp port or muscat
2 tsp castor sugar
black muscatel grapes

Cut a small hole in the end of the cantaloupe and retain the 'plug'.

Using a long-handled spoon (such as a parfait spoon), scoop out the seeds and discard. Pour port or muscat into the melon, seal with the plug and swish the liquid about. Chill melon for an hour or so, swirling port or muscat around from time to time. Cut into wedges and spoon on any juices. Garnish with grapes and leaves. (Do not serve melon too cold – it is at its best very lightly chilled.)

A SUMMER DELIGHT

As well as being 'almost healthy', this menu has the advantage of being prepared well in advance – a great help in hot weather, and for those of us who like to entertain sometimes during the week.

The Soda Bread can be quickly made at the last minute, if preferred, but you will find that it does reheat quite well.

Low in fats, and with chicken as the meat dish, this makes a light and tasty lunch or dinner menu, either for entertaining or for a pleasant family meal.

COLD ZUCCHINI AND RED CAPSICUM
SOUP WITH CUMIN

WHOLEMEAL SODA BREAD

MUSTARD COATED SPATCHCOCK OR
CHICKEN

MUSHROOM AND MIXED GREEN SALAD

POTATO SALAD OR PREFERRED SALAD*

GRATINEE OF SUMMER FRUITS WITH
CREME ECOSSAISE

COLD ZUCCHINI AND RED CAPSICUM SOUP WITH CUMIN

Serves 4–5

As well as its wonderful flavour, this recipe is a blessing for those desperate home gardeners whose crop of zucchini proliferates daily!

The roasting of the capsicums adds a distinctive flavour and aroma to the dish. To make peeling easy, slip the well charred capsicum into a plastic bag, seal it and wait 20 minutes. The skin peels off like magic!

2½–3 cups chopped, peeled zucchini
3 cups chicken stock
4 red capsicum, roasted
½ cup plain yoghurt (low-fat preferably)
1½ tsp ground cumin
julienned zucchini peel for garnish
wholemeal bread croutons

In a large saucepan, combine zucchini pulp and stock. Bring to the boil and simmer for 10 minutes. Add 2 cups of water, boil for 15 minutes and allow to cool. In a blender or food processor, purée the mixture with the roasted capsicum, yoghurt and cumin until the soup is smooth.

Transfer to a bowl and chill, covered, for at least 1 hour.

Divide soup among chilled bowls and sprinkle each serving with some of the julienned peel and croutons.

MUSTARD COATED SPATCHCOCK

Serves 4

I love this recipe and find it is always a popular addition to a picnic basket. It is a useful buffet dish, too – quick to prepare, and usually quickly eaten by hungry guests!

2 small spatchcock or 1 medium roasting chicken

COATING

2 tbsp coarse grained French mustard
2 tbsp lemon juice
2 tbsp light soy sauce
2 tbsp reduced cream
2 tbsp fine wholemeal breadcrumbs
1 tsp fresh thyme, chopped or ½ tsp dried thyme
pepper

Cut spatchcocks into halves or chicken into quarters and remove skin and any visible fat. Finely crumb one slice of wholemeal bread, crusts removed.

Place breadcrumbs and all other coating ingredients into a small bowl and mix until well blended. Spoon coating generously over the spatchcock or chicken portions; arrange portions on a shallow, lightly buttered oven tray and bake in a preheated moderate oven for about 45 minutes, or until meat juices run clear when flesh is pierced with a fine skewer. During cooking time, spoon over the poultry any mustard coating which runs into the pan.

To serve, arrange serving portions on a heated platter and spoon over any pan juices. Garnish with fresh lemon slices and fresh thyme sprigs.

Serve with a French salad, green beans or broccoli and tiny new potatoes. If preferred, accompany only with Mushroom and Mixed Green Salad.

Chicken may also be served cold. This cooks well, too, in a covered barbecue.

MUSHROOM AND MIXED GREEN SALAD

Serves 4

An excellent salad to serve with grilled or cold meats. I have used yoghurt in this version, but light sour cream may be substituted.

12 button mushrooms, sliced
1 tbsp lemon juice
¾ tsp sugar
¼ tsp salt
black pepper
3 spring onions, very finely sliced
2 tbsp unflavoured yoghurt
2 cups mesculn* or mixed lettuce leaves
French dressing (see recipe p 53)
very finely chopped parsley

Slice mushrooms wafer thin and place into a bowl with the lemon juice, sugar, salt, pepper and spring onions.

Allow to stand for about 1 hour, then stir in yoghurt.

Place mesculn or torn lettuce into a bowl and toss with the mushroom salad. Sprinkle with dressing and serve at once.

*Mesculn is a mixture of various salad greens picked and sold while they are still tiny. Better fruiterers often carry this now. An alternative is to plant masses of salad greens yourself and prune them as you require them!

GRATINEE OF SUMMER FRUITS

Serves 4–6

I include here a recipe for a light custard sauce,
but as there is a dairy food in the first course, I
leave it to your own discretion as to whether or
not you serve it with the fruits.

1 cup strawberries, hulled and wiped
1 cup raspberries, hulled and wiped
1 cup ripe pineapple chunks
2 yellow peaches, peeled and sliced
1 cup small green grapes
½ cup honey
1 tbsp Grand Marnier or brandy (optional)

Combine all the fruits in a shallow ovenproof container,
preferably in a single layer. Mix together the honey and Grand
Marnier (warm the honey, if necessary) and pour it over the
fruits. Allow to stand for several hours or overnight, stirring
the fruits occasionally.

To serve, preheat a griller until red hot. Place the fruits
under it, but only until the top fruits brown a little.
(A sprinkling of castor sugar helps speed up this process, but
I can't claim that this is healthy!) The fruits may be served
warm or chilled.

One variation is to macerate the fruits in a bowl, then to
spoon them into a dish into which the Crème Ecossaise has
been poured first and place them under the griller.
Alternatively, the crème may be passed with the fruits,
allowing guests to choose for themselves.

CREME ECOSSAISE

About 1½ cups

Most 'serious' cooks would feel guilty about adding flour to a crème, but a variation of this recipe was used by the respected French chef and food writer, Edouard de Pomaine, so I feel it has earned its place in a cookbook for busy people – it is not temperamental, and will quickly thicken every time without risk of the sauce 'turning'.

3 egg yolks
¾ tsp plain flour
3–4 tsp castor sugar
1 vanilla bean or 3 drops of vanilla
300 ml fat-reduced milk

Place egg yolks, flour and sugar into a small bowl and mix with a whisk.

Boil milk with the vanilla bean (if using); remove from heat and cool for a few seconds – then remove bean. If using vanilla essence, add it now.

Pour the hot milk little by little into the egg yolk mixture and whisk all the time. Empty contents of the bowl into a saucepan and stir over a very low heat. The sauce will thicken rapidly; remove at once.

Pour into a bowl, cover with plastic film and allow to cool.

WHOLEMEAL SODA BREAD

4–6 wedges

Unlike some 'quickbreads' this loaf is still tender the day after it is baked – makes terrific crunchy toast too! For a lighter loaf, use half white flour.

2 cups plain wholemeal flour
little salt (optional)
¾ tsp bicarbonate of soda
30g butter or margarine
2 tbsp rolled oats
¾–1 cup buttermilk or sour milk
extra oatmeal

Sift flour, salt and soda into a bowl. Rub in butter until mixture is the consistency of coarse breadcrumbs. Add the oatmeal. Pour in sufficient buttermilk to make a soft dough and mix lightly.

Sprinkle oatmeal onto a board and lightly shape the dough into a round. Brush the top with any remaining buttermilk, sprinkle with remaining oatmeal and place onto a lightly floured scone tray. Slash a deep cross in the top of the loaf.

Bake in a 200°C oven for about 30 minutes, or until well risen and golden.

Serve warm or cold.

A PRETTY LIGHT MEAL

Whichever way you choose to interpret the title of this menu, it is both light and pretty – a pleasant late evening meal, or even late morning, when the soup could be eliminated.

Dessert is simply fresh fruit, so you could choose your own varieties, depending on preference and season.

A visit to your local healthfood store will offer a wide choice of flours, including the buckwheat you need for this menu.

CHICKEN, MUSHROOM AND EGG FLOWER SOUP

BUCKWHEAT BLINI WITH RED CAVIAR

SUMMER BOUQUET SALAD

MELON WEDGES WITH GRAPES AND RASPBERRIES*

CHICKEN, MUSHROOM AND EGG FLOWER SOUP

Serves 6

1 lt well flavoured chicken stock (see recipe p 133)
6 spring onions
125g button mushrooms, sliced
180g cooked chicken meat, chopped or slivered
2 eggs, well beaten
pepper
1 tbsp dry sherry (optional)
2 tsp soy sauce
few spring onion greens, cut lengthwise

Prepare homemade chicken stock by straining, chilling and removing every particle of fat from the surface.

Finely cut the white part of the spring onions, reserving greens for garnish. Prepare mushrooms and chicken. Bring stock to the boil and add the sliced spring onions and mushrooms. Simmer for approximately 3 minutes, then add the chopped chicken meat. Whip eggs until frothy, then add pepper. Stir stock rapidly until it swirls in the pan; quickly pour in egg whilst stirring steadily. Cook for a minute or two until egg fragments are cooked and separate. (Yes, it *should* look a little curdled.)

Add sherry and soy sauce to taste.

Split onion greens into shreds lengthwise and add to soup as garnish.

BUCKWHEAT BLINI WITH RED CAVIAR

Serves 6

15g compressed yeast
¼ cup lukewarm milk
½ tsp sugar
1 egg, separated
⅓ cup buckwheat flour (or wholemeal flour, if necessary)
1 tbsp melted butter (optional)
little butter or dairy spread
3 tbsp red caviar
3 tbsp light sour cream, plain yoghurt or buttermilk
fresh dill sprigs or watercress

In a small bowl, mix together yeast, milk and sugar. Beat the egg yolk and add the yeast mixture, flour and melted butter. Cover and allow to stand for 3 hours or until batter doubles in bulk.

In a small bowl, beat the egg white until stiff, stir the batter (it will settle as it stands) and fold in beaten egg white.

Heat a heavy frying pan, brush with a little butter or dairy spread and drop 1 tablespoon of batter into the pan. Cook blini until browned underneath, then turn and brown other side. Continue until all batter is used.

Top each blini with a portion of the red caviar and a spoonful of the sour cream, yoghurt or buttermilk. Garnish with fresh dill or cress sprigs.

Note: Lumpfish roe may be substituted for caviar for a more economical dish.

The saltiness of *any* type of caviar, or its substitute, is sometimes a problem – just as well it is such an expensive, and therefore self-limiting, ingredient! However, I use the Australian/Atlantic salmon roe now (sparingly – it is not cheap) and find it has a delicate and less salty flavour.

SUMMER BOUQUET SALAD

This pretty and delicious salad needs young
greens to achieve the best results. If you grow
your own herbs – and I hope you do! – you'll
have no trouble in harvesting enough flowers for
your ingredients. Otherwise, just plant the
chives, nasturtiums, and borage in your
flowerbeds and you can enjoy their flavour as
well as beauty. Quantities are only approximate
– 'mix and match' your own leafy salad
ingredients.

2 cups small red mignonette lettuce leaves
2 witloof
2 cups tiny curly endive leaves
2 cups tiny spinach leaves
2 cups small, soft butter lettuce leaves
1 cup watercress sprigs
few nasturtium flowers (use leaves as well)
handful chive flowers
few borage flowers
chive wisps

DRESSING

5 tbsp light olive oil (or preferred salad oil)
3 tsp white wine vinegar
1 tsp raspberry vinegar
pepper
little salt (optional)
touch of sugar

Prepare the greens by rinsing well and removing stalks. Pat or shake as dry as possible and place into a crisper until ready to prepare the salad. Very lightly rinse and pat dry the flowers – they may be placed in the crisper with the greens. Arrange the greens on a platter and garnish with the flowers.

Just before serving, lightly sprinkle on dressing. Pour remainder into a jug and pass separately. (Cover and chill any remaining dressing for future use.)

To make dressing, combine all ingredients in a jar and shake vigorously.

If you are just in the process of discovering the delights of olive oil and feel a little tentative about using it too lavishly, I suggest you start using the extra light olive oil. Although it is recommended for frying, I feel its delicacy offers a gentle introduction to the distinctive flavour of olive oils.

A VERY CASUAL PICNIC

I'd jump at an invitation to share this simple lunch! Especially if it was to be eaten in the country on an early autumn day.

For those on low fat diets, substitute a non-fat salad dressing for the olive oil and French dressing, and serve a little skim milk cottage cheese instead of the cream cheeses. These are the small but significant compromises which create the illusion of being able to enjoy a normal eating programme.

PAN BAGNA

PICKLED OR HARD BOILED EGGS (for those not on low cholesterol diets)

QUARTERED LETTUCE SALAD WITH FRENCH DRESSING*

CARROT AND CELERY STICKS*

INDIVIDUALLY WRAPPED BEL PAESE CREAM CHEESES† WITH DRIED FIGS AND WALNUTS*

FRESH PEARS*

CHILLED DRY WHITE WINE* (either with soda water or 'straight')

MINERAL WATER*

†This mild-flavoured creamy cheese, from the Lombardy region of Italy, may be substituted with a low-fat cheese or one of the mild-flavoured Swiss cheeses.

PAN BAGNA

Serves 4–6

I'm mad about this simple Mediterranean 'sandwich' for which there seems to be countless versions – Elizabeth David offers three in her fabulous book *Summer Cooking*!

This is my own interpretation – and don't forget it's messy to eat, so serve it only to family and good friends.

1 long, flattish loaf of wholemeal bread
little light olive oil
1 clove garlic, halved
3 or 4 ripe tomatoes, thickly sliced
few button mushrooms, sliced
1 small can red salmon or tuna, well drained and
  flaked, or cooked chicken
few black olives, stoned and slivered
2–3 cooked or canned artichoke hearts, drained and
  quartered
black pepper

Cut the loaf in half lengthwise and sprinkle the surface with olive oil. Rub the cut bread generously with the cut garlic clove and discard garlic. Arrange all the ingredients on the base of the loaf and then replace the top. Wrap firmly in foil or plastic wrap and place under a heavy weight for an hour.

Unwrap and cut into thick slices and serve as a casual lunch – terrific for picnics.

PICKLED EGGS

This traditional English pub delicacy adds a piquant touch to any meal. They may be used within a day or so or may be allowed to mellow (or rather, sharpen!) in the spicy vinegar for up to 1 month. Sometimes they are kept very much longer, but 1 month is what I consider to be a reasonable length of time for them.

If you prefer a milder vinegar solution, dilute it with water before boiling with the chosen herbs and spices. If fresh herbs are unavailable, use ½ teaspoon of each of them dried.

12 hardboiled eggs (as fresh as possible), shelled
1 lt best quality white wine vinegar
1 tsp lightly crushed peppercorns
3 whole cloves
1 tsp mustard seeds
1 bay leaf
1 large sprig thyme
few sprigs parsley
1 sprig oregano

Prepare eggs and set aside.

Combine vinegar and all other ingredients, except eggs, in a non-corrosive saucepan and bring to the boil. Reduce heat and simmer for about 20 minutes.

Place eggs into jar, pour over vinegar and spices and herbs. Cool, then seal the jar. Store in a cool place and use as required.

THE PLEASURES OF AUTUMN

At this time of year we are able to enjoy the abundance of vegetables for which we have waited all summer.

Take advantage of this 'harvest time', and of the cooler weather – we can begin to enjoy again the heartier foods we have avoided during the hot days of summer.

This menu begins with a sturdy soup, high in fibre and nutrients, and is followed by a savoury tart which allows us to use an abundance of autumn produce. And who can resist the temptation of luscious figs, sharpened with a few late raspberries and sweetened with a little crab-apple jelly? All these palate-tingling delights – and 'almost healthy' as well!

AUTUMN HARVEST PISTOU

BUTTON SQUASH, APPLE AND ONION TART

CARROT AND ORANGE SALAD WITH CASHEWS

SALAD OF MIXED GREENS*

FIG FLOWERS WITH FRAGRANT RASPBERRIES

AUTUMN HARVEST PISTOU

Serves 6

175g lima beans
2 medium onions
1 tbsp fresh thyme leaves or 1 tsp dried thyme
2 garlic cloves
2 tsp olive oil
½ cup diced white turnip or parsnip
2 medium carrots, thickly sliced
2 celery stalks
5 cups chicken stock
1 large tomato, peeled and chopped or 1 cup canned
  Italian tomatoes, drained and chopped
1 medium zucchini, halved lengthwise, then cut into
  thick slices
2 cups chopped spinach
1 tsp salt (optional)
freshly ground pepper
finely chopped parsley

Cover the beans with cold water and soak overnight. (Alternatively, cover the beans with 10 cm of cold water and bring to the boil over high heat. Boil for 2 minutes, remove from heat and let the beans soak, covered, for 1 hour.)

Drain the beans, place in a medium saucepan and cover with cold water. Halve one of the onions and add to the beans. Add 1 teaspoon of the thyme leaves and 1 garlic clove. Bring to the boil over high heat; reduce heat and simmer until the beans are cooked through and tender, about 1 hour. Drain the beans and discard the onion and garlic clove. (The recipe may be prepared to this point 1 day in advance and then chilled.)

Dice the remaining onion and finely chop the remaining garlic. In a large, heavy pan or casserole, warm the olive oil over moderately high heat. Add the diced onion, garlic, turnip or parsnip, carrots and celery. Reduce the heat to low and cook the vegetables until onions are translucent, about 7 minutes. Stir from time to time.

Pour in the chicken stock and remaining thyme and simmer the soup over moderately low heat until the vegetables are just tender, about 25 minutes. Add tomato, zucchini and spinach and cook for 1 minute only.

Transfer the soup to a serving bowl to cool a little, or serve hot. When the soup has cooled, season with pepper. Serve at room temperature, sprinkled with some freshly chopped parsley.

BUTTON SQUASH, APPLE AND ONION TART

Serves 6

Of course it is mainly the pastry which is the 'slightly less than healthy' element in this dish. If you wish, select a low-fat pastry or even eliminate it and cook the filling as a crustless flan in a pie plate or solid based flan.

SHELL

short crust pastry
raw rice for weighting shell

1 tbsp extra-light olive oil
750g onions, halved lengthwise and thinly sliced
2 garlic cloves, very finely chopped
2 tsp finely chopped fresh sage or ¾ tsp dried sage
½ tps fresh thyme leaves, crumbled or ¼ tsp dried thyme
¼ cup light cream
1 large golden delicious apple
250g button squash, peeled, halved lengthwise and thinly sliced
1 tbsp cream, yoghurt or milk
fresh sage sprigs for garnish

Make pastry shell by rolling out dough thinly on a lightly floured board and fitting it into 25 cm square flan, leaving 5 cm overhang. Fold the overhang inward onto the sides of the shell and press it firmly against the side of the tin. Prick the shell lightly with a fork and chill for 30 minutes. Line the shell with waxed paper, fill with rice and bake the shell in lower shelf of a preheated 210°C oven for 15 minutes. Remove the rice and paper carefully and bake the shell for 5–8 minutes further, or until it is golden. Allow to cool in the flan.

In a large, heavy pan, heat the oil until hot but not smoking, stir in the onions and garlic with pepper to taste and cook, covered, over low heat for 20–25 minutes, or until the onions are softened, stirring often.

Add the chopped sage, thyme and cream. Bring the liquid to the boil and simmer, stirring occasionally for 3–5 minutes, or until it is slightly thickened. Let the onion mixture cool. Spoon the onion evenly into the pastry shell. Peel and halve the apple lengthwise; core it and slice it very thinly crosswise. Arrange the apple and the button squash slices over the onion mixture, overlapping them and brush them with the cream, yoghurt or milk.

Bake the tart in the upper third of a preheated 190°C oven for 15 minutes, then cover the tart with foil and bake it for 30 minutes more, or until the button squash is tender. Let the tart cool in the flan tin, then remove the flan tin and transfer it to a platter. Serve the tart warm or at room temperature, garnished with sage sprigs if desired.

Serves 8–10 as a first course or 4–6 as a luncheon.

CARROT AND ORANGE SALAD WITH CASHEWS

Serves 4–5

4 large juicy carrots, scrubbed and grated
2 oranges, peeled and segmented
2–3 spring onions, finely chopped or shredded
½ cup raisins
freshly ground pepper
French dressing (see recipe p 53)
shredded coconut (optional)
julienned orange rind
toasted cashew nuts

Combine carrots, orange segments, spring onions, raisins and pepper. Pour on dressing, toss well and sprinkle with shredded coconut, orange rind and cashew nuts.

Salad may be served in a bowl, or arranged on young spinach leaves or other greens on a platter.

FIG FLOWERS WITH FRAGRANT RASPBERRIES

Serves 4

4 large luscious figs
1 cup ripe raspberries
2–3 tbsp homemade crab-apple jelly or red currant
*   jelly*
scented geranium leaves and flowers (if available)

Trim stems of the figs so they will stand flat on the base. Split the fruit open from blossom end to stem, so that petals are formed without cutting right through to the base. Arrange them on individual plates and chill.

Melt the jelly in a small saucepan, adding a touch of water if necessary. (If you have a rose-scented geranium bush, wash and crush a few leaves and add them, but remove them after the jelly has melted.)

Cool the jelly a little, then toss in the raspberries, stirring very, very gently to avoid crushing them. Spoon the raspberries into the centre of each fig and garnish with leaves and flowers.

If you have plenty of raspberries, serve a sauce of crushed berries with the dessert.

A strawberry purée is another pleasant variation.

LUNCH UNDER THE TREES

A few weeks ago I was invited to lunch by an old friend. There were three guests, and we shared a wonderful, simple meal under a big, old tree in a rambling country-style garden in the suburbs. It was a beautiful autumn day and the filtered sunlight and the sounds of birds and bees turned the meal into a special occasion.

This menu tries to recapture the spirit of that day if not the actual food which was served. We did have open sandwiches, followed by delicious fruits, and of course you can put together your own favourite combinations to achieve the same results.

A SELECTION OF OPEN SANDWICHES
SERVED ON VARIOUS BREADS

FRESH FRUIT SALAD*

SUGGESTED SANDWICH TOPPINGS

- Lettuce, wedge of fresh pineapple, tiny tomatoes or sliced tomato, sliced mushroom, onion

- Cos lettuce, rolled ham, tomato wedges, dab of grainy mustard

- Mix greens, baby tomatoes, slice of avocado, squeeze of lemon juice, olives

- Greens, scoop of cottage cheese, chopped herbs or watercress, julienned carrot, celery

- Greens, shredded roast chicken, little pickle or chutney, small tomatoes, spring onion

A BUFFET SPREAD

This is a simple buffet consisting of a hearty soup, several 'snacky' items and a sweet dessert. Apart from the tuna in one dish, this menu would be perfectly acceptable for vegetarians. The recipes could all be used individually, of course, to provide pre-dinner snacks with drinks, or the soup could be served as part of a soup and sandwich lunch. These are useful, 'almost healthy' recipes to have tucked away in your files.

GOLDEN SOUP WITH BROWN RICE

HOMEMADE LIPTAUER CHEESE

HERBED MUSHROOM PATE

CRISPY TUNA ROLLS

MINTED BROWN RICE SALAD

ALMOST HEALTHY BAKLAVA

GOLDEN SOUP WITH BROWN RICE

Serves 6

250g soya beans or 1 can prepared beans
250g yellow dried peas
1 large onion, chopped
1 large carrot, chopped
1 large potato, chopped
500g tomatoes, skinned and chopped or 1 can
*   tomatoes, chopped*
2 sticks celery, chopped
2 tsp fresh chopped oregano or 1 tsp dried oregano
parsley
2 bay leaves
1 clove garlic, chopped
little salt
pepper
1.5lt water or stock
6 tbsp cooked brown rice, hot

Cook beans and peas until tender. (Soak overnight to speed up this process.) Chop onion and brown lightly in a little oil. Combine all ingredients and allow to simmer until thick and well cooked.

Put mixture through a blender or mouli. Serve very hot and spoon a tablespoon of hot brown rice into each bowl.

Garnish with a little extra chopped parsley. If no cheese is served with the main course, a sprinkling of grated tasty cheese adds flavour and interest to this soup.

HOMEMADE LIPTAUER CHEESE

Makes approximately 1 cup

This recipe, based on a delicious, traditional Hungarian cheese spread, offers a wonderful flavour.

125g cottage cheese
1 tbsp dairy spread or margarine (optional)
2 tsp chopped capers, rinsed and drained well
2 tsp sweet paprika
2 tsp finely chopped chives
1 tsp hot mustard
1 tsp anchovy paste or essence
freshly ground pepper

Beat together cheese and dairy spread or margarine, then beat in the remaining ingredients. Cover and chill for at least 2 hours before serving.

Serve as a dip or a little first course with vegetable crudites, or as a filling for fresh mushrooms.

Note: If a more robust flavour is preferred, add a little hot paprika or chilli powder.

Opposite: A Summer Delight, see page 24
Overleaf left: A Pretty Light Meal, see page 31
Overleaf right: A Very Casual Picnic, see page 36
Opposite page 51: The Pleasures of Autumn, see page 39

HERBED MUSHROOM PATE

Serves 10

1 small onion, chopped
3 spring onions, chopped
1 stalk celery, chopped
1½ garlic cloves, finely chopped
125g unsalted butter
500g mushrooms, thinly sliced
1 cup chopped walnuts
1 tbsp fresh basil, chopped or 2 tsp dried basil
2 tsp fresh thyme or 1 tsp dried thyme
1 tsp fresh oregano or ½ tsp dried oregano
¾ tsp fresh rosemary, ground or ⅓ tsp dried rosemary
360g cream cheese, cut into pieces and softened
⅓ cup fine fresh wholemeal breadcrumbs
¼ tsp black pepper
1 large egg, lightly beaten

In a large pan, cook the onion, spring onions, celery, garlic
and butter over moderately low heat until the vegetables are
softened. Increase the heat to moderately high, add mushrooms
and walnuts in batches, and cook the mixture, stirring for
several minutes after each addition. Add herbs and cook the
mixture, stirring for 10 minutes, or until the liquid from the
mushrooms is evaporated. Stir in the cream cheese and mix
until well combined. Add breadcrumbs and pepper, and stir
well. Allow the mixture to cool to room temperature. In a
food processor, chop the mixture in batches; spoon into a bowl
and stir in the egg.

Spoon the mixture into a buttered loaf tin 23 × 10 × 6.5cm
and tap the pan firmly on a bench to expel any air bubbles.
Cover the mixture with wax paper and foil, pulling tightly
to edge of pan. Bake mixture in a preheated 180°C oven for
1 hour. Allow the pâté to cool, cover and chill overnight.

Remove foil and paper, run a knife around the edge of the
pâté and invert onto a plate.

Cut the pâté into slices to serve or use to stuff fresh
mushrooms.

CRISPY TUNA ROLLS

Makes 16–18 small rolls

1 can 425g tuna, drained
2 large hard boiled eggs, very finely chopped
½ cup chopped or shredded lettuce
¼ tsp curry powder
plenty of pepper
1 tbsp mayonnaise
125g puff pastry
egg yolk

Flake tuna and mix with chopped eggs, lettuce, curry powder and pepper. Blend lightly, but thoroughly. Fold in the mayonnaise.

Roll pastry very thinly, or use pre-rolled pastry, and cut pastry in half. Place filling down one edge and roll up; brush edge with egg yolk and press lightly to seal. Cut into small rolls and prick each several times with a fork. Brush tops with egg yolk and arrange rolls in a lightly greased scone tray. Chill until ready to bake.

Cook in 225°C oven for about 10 minutes.

Serve as a tasty snack, as a nibble with drinks or as a hearty accompaniment to a salad. If preferred, bake the rolls whole, then cut into serving portions.

MINTED BROWN RICE SALAD

Serves 6–8

2 cups brown rice, cooked
⅓ cup chopped mint
¾ cup cherry tomatoes, halved
freshly ground pepper
1 cup peas, cooked
½ cup freshly chopped parsley
1 grated carrot
1–2 tsp grated fresh ginger root
2 tbsp desiccated coconut, lightly toasted
dressing

Mix together all salad ingredients, except coconut and dressing. To serve, pour dressing through salad and mix lightly. Serve sprinkled with coconut and garnish with mint leaves.

FRENCH DRESSING

1 clove garlic, crushed or very finely chopped
2 tbsp lemon juice
pinch raw sugar
little black pepper
4 tbsp light olive oil
pinch mustard

Combine all ingredients in a screw top jar and shake well. Keep chilled.

This quantity will provide more than the rice salad requires as 2–3 tablespoons should be sufficient to moisten it.

ALMOST HEALTHY BAKLAVA

Serves 8–10

I concede that it is impossible to totally 'healthify' this delicious Greek cake with its essential pastry and sweet syrup; however, with a bit of ingredient juggling, it does become more acceptable, and with little flavour compromise.

½ cup melted unsalted butter
500g filo pastry
1 cup finely chopped walnuts
1 cup finely chopped, toasted and skinned hazelnuts
good pinch ground cloves
2 tsp cinnamon
2 tbsp wheatgerm
½ cup lecithin meal
¼ cup sugar
honey syrup as per recipe

Lightly butter a large, shallow ovenproof dish or baking tray and place 8 sheets of filo pastry separately into the dish, brushing each sheet with the melted butter.

Mix together nuts, spices, wheatgerm, lecithin and sugar and spread half of this mixture over the pastry. Top with another 2 sheets of filo, brushing each with the butter. Spread remaining nut mixture over pastry and add another 6–8 sheets, brushing each with the melted butter. Trim off any overhanging edges and brush top with butter. Score through a few top layers with a sharp knife and sprinkle surface lightly with a little water to create a crisp surface.

Bake low in a moderate oven for approximately 30 minutes, then move up in the oven and cook for a further 30 minutes. (If top cooks too quickly, cover with a piece of foil or brown paper.) While baklava cooks, make up the syrup and allow this to cool.

Remove baklava from oven and cut into diamond shapes. Whilst still hot, spoon syrup over top. Allow to stand for at least several hours, or overnight, before serving as an afternoon tea treat or as a dessert course.

HONEY SYRUP

1 cup hot water
¾ cup honey
3 whole cloves
cinnamon stick
1 tbsp lemon juice (or more to taste)

Mix together, bring to the boil and cook together for 10 minutes. Strain.

A STURDY MEAL

I keep emphasising that 'almost healthy' eating depends on quantity as well as on the ingredients in the dishes. Because the polenta recipe is a hearty one, I feel that it could be extended to six – however, if your appetite is hearty too, it might be necessary to increase the size of this recipe to feed that number. No problem, just increase all ingredients by half...

I have suggested little bocconini cheeses for the first course, but, if you have any difficulty in locating these, settle for little mozzarellas which are equally as good.

I am always reluctant to substitute dried basil for fresh, so suggest you use a different herb – perhaps mint or marjoram – if basil is out of season.

TOMATO, BOCCONINI AND BASIL SALAD

BAKED POLENTA WITH A TRIO OF
MUSHROOMS AND TOMATO SAUCE

PASSIONFRUIT CREAMS WITH FRESH
RASPBERRY COULIS

TOMATO, BOCCONINI AND BASIL SALAD

Serves 6

2 small bocconini or mozzarella cheeses, sliced
3 large tomatoes, sliced
little French dressing
black pepper
fresh basil

Arrange overlapping slices of cheese and tomato on a serving plate. Add chopped basil and black pepper to a little French dressing and place on the plate in a small bowl or jug.

Garnish the salad with fresh herb leaves and add a sprinkling of black pepper.

Best served at room temperature.

BAKED POLENTA WITH A TRIO OF MUSHROOMS AND TOMATO SAUCE

Serves 4–6

Not everybody shares my enthusiasm for polenta, but I love it and recommend this version as a very tasty and healthy addition to anyone's diet. If dried mushrooms are a problem to find, use all fresh mushrooms instead.

SAUCE

¼ cup dried mushrooms (about 25g)
½ cup water
1 tbsp olive oil
½ cup chopped onion
2 tbsp diced carrot
2 tbsp diced celery
1 clove garlic, finely chopped
185g fresh field mushrooms, stems trimmed and sliced
90g oyster mushrooms (including stems), cut into slices
¼ cup dry red wine
1 tsp fresh thyme leaves or ½ tsp dried thyme
freshly ground pepper
480g can Roma tomatoes (liquid reserved), chopped
fresh parsley

POLENTA

olive oil
6 tbsp freshly grated Parmesan cheese
1 cup cold skim milk
1 cup yellow cornmeal
1½ cups well skimmed chicken stock
1½ cups water

To make sauce, combine dry mushrooms and ½ cup water in a small, heavy saucepan. Bring to the boil, reduce heat, cover and simmer for 5 minutes. Remove from heat, cover and allow to stand for 5 minutes. Remove mushrooms and strain liquid through a fine seive. If less than 3 tablespoons of liquid, add sufficient water to measure 3 tablespoons. Set liquid aside. Chop mushrooms and set aside.

Heat oil in a heavy non-stick pan over medium low heat. Add onion, carrot and celery and sauté until golden, about 9 minutes. Add garlic and sauté for 1 minute. Stir in fresh mushrooms and reserved liquid. Increase heat to medium and sauté until mushrooms are tender and most of the liquid has evaporated.

Push mushrooms to side of pan. Increase heat and add wine. Bring to the boil, then stir in mushrooms. Reduce heat to medium and stir until wine reduces slightly, about 5 minutes. Stir in dried mushrooms, thyme and pepper and mix well. Add tomatoes with liquid and bring to the boil stirring constantly. Reduce heat and simmer until sauce is slightly thickened and chunky, about 12 minutes. Stir in parsley and adjust seasoning. (Can be prepared 1 day ahead, cooled, then covered and chilled.)

For polenta, preheat oven to 200°C and lightly brush sides and base of a 20 cm square baking dish with oil. Sprinkle with 1 tablespoon Parmesan.

Pour the milk into a bowl, gradually stir in the cornmeal and set aside.

Bring stock and water to the boil in a large heavy saucepan and add the cornmeal mixture. Reduce heat and cook, stirring constantly, or at least fairly frequently (!), until the polenta is stiff and pulls away from the sides of the saucepan – this should take about 15 minutes. Stir in 4 tablespoons Parmesan.

Spoon polenta into the prepared dish and sprinkle with the rest of the Parmesan. (Dish may be prepared to this stage one day ahead.) Bake polenta until edges begin to brown, about 30 minutes. Remove from heat and stand on a rack for about 10 minutes.

Reheat sauce if necessary. Cut polenta into portions and place onto heated plates. Top with sauce and serve at once.

PASSIONFRUIT CREAMS WITH FRESH RASPBERRY COULIS

Serves 6

A glorious way of using the super abundance of passionfruit some of us enjoy each summer!

3 eggs
2 egg yolks
1 tbsp icing sugar
1½ cups passionfruit pulp
2–3 tsp lemon juice
750 ml sieved raspberry purée
additional raspberries for garnish
mint leaves or sprigs

Whisk eggs, yolks and sugar until thick and pale. Bring passionfruit pulp to the boil and pour, whisking constantly, into the egg mixture. Add lemon juice and whisk again until well blended.

Preheat oven to 180°C.

Lightly butter 6 individual moulds and fill with mixture. Place side by side in a large roasting pan and add hot water to come halfway up the moulds. Cook for about 20 minutes in the centre of the oven. Turn off heat and allow to cool in the oven with the door open.

One hour before serving, chill 6 dessert plates. When creams are cool, remove from moulds, place onto chilled plates and put in refrigerator.

When ready to serve, spoon raspberry coulis around. Garnish with a mint sprig and a few whole berries and serve immediately.

AN ITALIAN DINNER

The flavour of Italian food excites most 'food-ies', but the health conscious among us worry a bit about the sheer volume and high fat content of many Mediterranean dishes. However, with a little adaptation, Italian dishes can become most acceptable for an 'almost healthy' lifestyle.

I hope this menu will offer encouragement for modifying those of your own traditional Italian favourites that have been discarded as being inappropriate for healthy eating.

ROMAN CONSOMME

BRAISED VEAL SHANKS WITH
GREMOLADA

NOODLES OR BOILED RICE*

GREEN VEGETABLES (SUCH AS
BROCCOLI, BEANS, BABY BROAD BEANS,
ZUCCHINI ETC.)*

ITALIAN TOMATO SALAD WITH
ANCHOVY DRESSING

ITALIAN BREAD*

RUBY POACHED APPLES WITH SPICED
WINE SYRUP

ROMAN CONSOMME

Serves 4

4 cups rich, clear chicken stock (see recipe p 133)
1½ tsp very finely chopped fresh oregano or ½ tsp dried
 oregano
2 tbsp very finely chopped parsley
1 large egg
2 tbsp lemon juice
1 tbsp finely grated Romano or similar cheese
freshly ground pepper

In a large saucepan, bring the stock and oregano to the boil.
Whisk together egg, parsley, lemon juice and cheese until
fluffy. Pour egg mixture into boiling stock and whisk lightly
to form the 'little rags' which gives this soup its Italian name
of 'stracciatella'. Add pepper to taste and serve immediately in
heated bowls.

A little chopped parsley may be added as a garnish.

BRAISED VEAL SHANKS WITH GREMOLADA

Serves 4

Of course this is a version of the traditional Italian osso bucco, but with a few modifications. The delicious 'oozy' marrow which exudes from the bones when they are sawn across and cooked has to be sacrificed, but with this small concession the dish becomes a delicious addition to our 'almost healthy' programme.

1 large veal shank or 2 smaller ones
1 tbsp extra-light olive oil
2 medium white onions, chopped
2 medium carrots, chopped
2 stalks celery, sliced
½ tsp chopped garlic
5 large fresh tomatoes, chopped or 450g can Roma
  tomatoes, chopped
1 cup rich beef or veal stock
1 cup dry white wine
2 tbsp chopped parsley
1 tsp freshly chopped basil or ½ teaspoon dried basil
½ tsp fresh thyme leaves or ⅓ teaspoon dried thyme
1 bay leaf
freshly ground pepper
hot boiled rice

GREMOLADA

2 tbsp finely grated lemon rind
2 tbsp finely chopped parsley
1 tsp very finely chopped garlic

Carefully remove all meat from the shank and cut into large cubes. Heat oil in a non-stick pan and slowly brown the meat, in batches. Transfer meat to a large, lidded saucepan. Sauté onion, carrot, celery and garlic in the pan for a few minutes, then add to the veal in the saucepan. Stir in chopped tomatoes and juice (if canned; if using fresh tomatoes, add ½ cup tomato juice or water), stock, wine, herbs and pepper. Bring to the boil, cover, reduce heat and simmer for 1 hour or until veal is tender. While veal cooks, prepare the gremolada: combine lemon rind, parsley and garlic and mix together.

When veal is cooked, remove the bay leaf. If a thick sauce is preferred, remove one cup of vegetables and liquid from the saucepan, and purée. Return to saucepan and stir lightly. Sprinkle on the gremolada and simmer saucepan to reheat and to blend flavours.

Spoon meat and vegetables onto heated platters and serve with boiled rice and vegetables. Accompany with the Italian Tomato Salad – wonderful eating when the salad is spooned onto the plate after the veal has been eaten! Juices should be mopped up afterwards with good Italian bread – but of course the weight conscious must resist this tempation!

ITALIAN TOMATO SALAD

Serves 4

4–5 large, ripe tomatoes
1 medium onion, preferably red
freshly ground black pepper
chopped fresh basil

ANCHOVY DRESSING

3 tbs light olive oil
3 anchovies
1 tbsp red wine vinegar (or balsamic vinegar)
black pepper
basil leaves

Slice tomatoes thickly and arrange on a platter. Slice onions very thinly and scatter onto the tomatoes. Sprinkle with pepper. Cover and chill.

To make dressing, soak anchovies in milk for an hour or so, then drain and pat dry. (This reduces the saltiness of the anchovies.) Chop them finely or mash well. Combine oil, vinegar, anchovies and pepper and whisk together.

Drizzle the dressing onto the tomato salad, sprinkle with chopped fresh basil.

Serve garnished with whole fresh basil leaves. (Left over dressing will keep, covered, for a week under refrigeration.)

RUBY POACHED APPLES WITH SPICED WINE SYRUP

Serves 4

4 small, firm cooking apples
1½ cups rosé wine (any light red wine will do)
½ cup water
3 tbsp honey
1 small cinnamon stick
1 thick lemon slice
1 large strip orange peel
3 whole cloves
julienned orange and lemon rind
mint leaves
egg white
little castor sugar

Core the apples from the 'blossom' end, leaving the core intact. Peel apples and place into a bowl of acidulated water to prevent discoloration (2 cups water to 1 tablespoon lemon juice).

Combine wine, water, honey, cinnamon stick, lemon slice, orange peel and cloves and cook over high heat for several minutes.

Drain apples and drop them into the syrup; bring back to the boil for 1 minute. Reduce heat and simmer gently, uncovered, for about 20 minutes or until apples are tender. (If apples are not colouring evenly, turn them gently during cooking time to ensure uniform colour.) Remove from heat.

Allow the apples to cool in the syrup, turning them often. Gently remove apples with a slotted spoon and place into a bowl.

Strain syrup and reduce to one-third of original volume. Pour syrup over apples and chill.

To serve, place apples onto individual plates and spoon on the syrup. Garnish with julienned citrus peel and sugared mint leaves. To make these, lightly brush well washed and dried mint leaves with a little lightly beaten egg white, then sprinkle with castor sugar.

A LITTLE LUNCH FOR SIX

Because both the main course and the dessert have a reasonably high fat level, the first course is a very light soup. There is also a choice of using milk rather than cream in the tartlet filling; although the filling will be a little less rich and smooth, the end result is still most acceptable.

Remember that you are in control of the size of the portions that are served, so serve small scoops of icecream and add extra fresh fruit. It is always important to remember that the *quantity* is a major factor in creating an 'almost healthy' eating programme.

THAI CHICKEN AND MUSHROOM SOUP

LATTICED BUTTERNUT TARTLETS IN
SUNFLOWER SEED CRUST

MIXED GREENS*

BANANA OR MANGO AND TOASTED
PECAN ICECREAM

OR

A SELECTION OF FRESH FRUITS*

THAI CHICKEN AND MUSHROOM SOUP

I guess the 'sinful' ingredient in this dish would have to be the nam pla – a very salty fish sauce which gives the soup its distinctive flavour. Don't leave it out – just eliminate salt from the rest of your meal.

1 clove garlic, crushed or very finely chopped
1 tbsp finely chopped fresh coriander leaves and stems
¼ tsp freshly ground black pepper
2 tsp vegetable oil
1 lt light chicken stock
125 g mushrooms, thinly sliced
2 tbsp nam pla (or anchovy essence if nam pla
  unavailable)
125 g chicken breasts, cut into fine strips
4 spring onions, thinly sliced

Combine the garlic, coriander and pepper in a mortar and pound. In a small frying pan, heat the oil over medium heat and when hot, sauté the garlic mixture for 1 minute. Remove the mixture from the heat and set aside.

Combine the stock, mushrooms, nam pla and the garlic mixture in a saucepan and simmer for 5 minutes. Add chicken and simmer only long enough to heat through. Sprinkle with spring onions.

Adjust seasoning and serve at once, garnished with a little fresh coriander if desired.

LATTICED BUTTERNUT TARTLETS IN SUNFLOWER SEED CRUST

Serves 6

CASES

sunflower seed pastry dough (see over page)
raw rice for weighting cases

FILLING

1 cup puréed steamed butternut pumpkin
¼ cup cream or unflavoured yoghurt or milk
1 large egg, lightly beaten
¼ tsp salt (optional)
¼ tsp pepper
125g thinly sliced Swiss-style cheese, cut into thin
   strips for the lattice topping

To make cases, roll out the dough thinly on a lightly floured surface; with a 11 cm round cutter, cut out 6 rounds, gathering and rerolling the scraps as necessary. Press each round into a fluted individual flan tin, prick the cases lightly with a fork and chill them for about 30 minutes. Line the shells with parchment, fill with rice and bake in a pan on the lower shelf of a preheated 220°C oven for 15 minutes. Remove rice and paper carefully and bake the cases for a further 5 minutes, or until they are golden. Cool the shells in the pans. (The cases may be made 1 day in advance and stored in an airtight container.)

To make filling, in a food processor or blender, blend the pumpkin with the cream or yoghurt, egg, salt (if using) and pepper. Divide the filling among the tartlet cases; smooth the surface and arrange 6 strips of Swiss-style cheese, trimming them to fit, in a lattice pattern across each tartlet.

Bake the tarts in an oven pan in the middle of a 190°C oven for 20–25 minutes, or until the filling is puffed slightly and the cheese melted.

Serve immediately or allow to cool to room temperature. Serve with undressed salad greens.

SUNFLOWER SEED PASTRY DOUGH

¼ cup roasted sunflower seeds
1 cup plain flour
4 tbsp cold unsalted butter, cut into cubes
2–3 tbsp iced water
little extra flour for dusting

In a food processor, grind the sunflower seeds finely and add 1 cup of flour. Add the butter and blend until mixture resembles coarse breadcrumbs. Transfer to a bowl and toss it with just enough iced water to form a dough. Knead the dough lightly with the heels of hands, distributing the butter evenly, for just a few seconds. Form dough into a ball, dust with additional flour and chill, wrapped in waxed paper, for at least 1 hour.

BANANA AND TOASTED PECAN ICE CREAM

Serves 8

At first sight, this looks too wicked even for an 'almost healthy' eating programme. However, when we divide it into eight portions it means that it works out at about 1½ tablespoons of cream and ½ tablespoon of sugar and ¼ of an egg per serving! Not bad really when it is balanced against the rest of the menu.

3 ripe bananas, mashed or 2 ripe mangoes, peeled and
  chopped
2 tsp lemon juice
⅓ cup milk
2 eggs, separated
¼ cup castor sugar
1 cup light cream
1 tsp vanilla essence
½ cup finely chopped toasted pecan nuts

Combine mashed bananas or mango pulp, lemon juice and milk in a basin and stir together until well mixed. Beat egg whites until stiff, add sugar and whip until thick and glossy. Beat egg yolks until thick; add cream and whip until thickened.

Fold together mashed bananas or mangoes, egg white mixture, beaten yolks and cream, vanilla and finely chopped pecan nuts. Pour into ice cream maker and process according to the maker's instructions. If a machine is not used, pour ice cream mixture into freezer trays and freeze until lightly frozen.

Serve with a fruit purée or sliced mango.

A TOUCH OF THE MIDDLE EAST

Loosely based on some of my own favourite Middle Eastern recipes, this menu is perfect for our 'almost healthy' eating philosophy. The saltiness of the olives will worry some, and other purists will be concerned about the butter on our pitas. Just substitute vegetable crudités or some other acceptable alternative for the olives, and serve the bread unbuttered if you prefer. You will still be able to enjoy a delicious meal.

A BOWL OF HERBED OLIVES

KOFTA SKEWERS WITH BASIL BUTTERED PITA BREAD

CHOPPED TOMATO AND ONION OR TABBOULEH*

EMERALD AND RUBY SALAD

SPICED KOSHAV

HERBED OLIVES

There is a lightly salted brand of bottled olives being imported at present; ask for these at Continental delicatessens. You can help reduce the saltiness of ordinary olives (and I like to use Calamata or Nicoise when I can get them) by soaking them overnight in cold water. If you do this once or twice, draining them well each time, you will certainly somewhat reduce the salt levels.

To make my herbed olives, I follow the method below.

500g black olives
sprigs of thyme, marjoram, oregano and rosemary
3 garlic cloves, peeled and quartered
extra-light olive oil

Place the olives into a bowl or jar. Add the herbs and garlic cloves and mix together. Pour on sufficient olive oil to cover, and allow to stand for several days. I keep mine for months like this, and just fish out the required amount of olives with a pierced-bowl wooden spoon. (It doesn't look as good, but a slotted spoon works just as well!) However, if you are reluctant to use the olive oil so generously, use the following technique. About 24 hours before you plan to serve the olives, place them into a bowl and add 2 tablespoons of extra-light olive oil. Add the herbs and garlic and mix together. Cover tightly and allow to stand.

KOFTA SKEWERS WITH BASIL BUTTERED PITA BREAD

Serves 6 as a light course

500g lean minced lamb
1 white onion, coarsely chopped
½ clove garlic, finely chopped or crushed
1 egg, lightly beaten
1 tsp ground cinnamon
pepper
olive oil

Mix together lamb, onion and garlic until well blended, then mix in egg, cinnamon and pepper. Mould meat mixture to a thickness of approximately 3.5 cm around wooden or bamboo satay sticks which have been soaked in cold water. Lightly brush meat with a little olive oil. Under a preheated griller, quickly brown meat on all sides (do not overcook). Serve at once, tucked into a homemade pita bread or a Lebanese flatbread, buttered lightly with Basil Butter.

Serve with chopped tomato and onion or Tabbouleh.

Lunch Under the Trees, see page 46

HOMEMADE PITA BREAD

30g compressed yeast
1 cup lukewarm water
1 tbsp oil
1 tsp sugar
3½–4 cups plain flour
1 tsp salt

In a large bowl, mix together the crumbled yeast, water, oil and sugar. Add 1½ cups of flour and beat for approximately 2 minutes. Using a wooden spoon, stir in enough flour to produce a soft dough. Add the remainder of the flour, work lightly, then turn on to a pastry board and knead until smooth and silky. Cover with a cloth and stand in a warm place until dough doubles in bulk.

Punch down, divide into 6 and roll each piece into a round about the size of a bread and butter plate. Arrange on lightly greased oven trays and allow to stand for about 45 minutes or until rounds have risen to twice their original height.

Bake in a preheated very hot oven 230°C for 8–10 minutes or until puffed golden. Remove pitas from trays, cool slightly, then place into plastic bags to prevent hardening.

These freeze well.

BASIL BUTTER

125g slightly softened unsalted butter
2 tbsp chopped fresh basil or 1 tbsp dried basil
good squeeze lemon
black pepper

Beat together all ingredients until well blended. Spread lightly onto pita bread for serving. Cover remaining butter and refrigerate for future use.

A Buffet Spread, see page 48

EMERALD AND RUBY SALAD

Serves 6

variety of lettuce leaves, well washed and dried
1 Continental cucumber
1 green capsicum
2 spring onions, chopped
finely chopped parsley

RUBY DRESSING

1 tbsp light olive oil
1 tbsp red wine vinegar
2 large, ripe tomatoes, peeled and seeded
2 tbsp chopped onion
1 tbsp fresh chopped basil or ½ tsp dried basil
pepper

Tear lettuce into pieces. Slice cucumber and capsicum.

Combine dressing ingredients in processor or blender and process coarsely. Pour dressing over salad and serve at once.

SPICED KOSHAV

Serves 6

This dessert – a longtime favourite with my friends – gets better as it matures. By the end of a week it is glorious. To extend it, or to offer a change of flavour, add a small can of unsweetened peaches and half a cup of their unsweetened liquid.

185g dried apricots
185g seeded raisins
125g plump stoned prunes
½ cup honey
1 thick slice of orange
peel of a lemon
1 cinnamon stick
4 cloves
½ tsp mixed ground spices
½ cup orange juice
1½ tbsp Grand Marnier (optional)

Place dried fruits into a bowl and pour on sufficient boiling water to barely cover. Cover bowl and allow to stand overnight.

Drain well next day and place fruits into a saucepan; add honey, orange slice, lemon peel, cinnamon stick and spices. Pour on just enough boiling water to cover and simmer very gently for about 30 minutes. Cool, pour in the orange juice and Grand Marnier (if using) and cover and chill for at least 24 hours.

Serve with a little plain yoghurt or sour cream.

A STYLISH DINNER PARTY

Not so long ago it would have been expected that one would serve rich and lavish courses for a dinner party. Nowadays that has changed completely and it is often a problem to accommodate the dietary preferences of guests – it always seems that at least one of them is following the latest 'healthy' diet. I have learnt now to check with friends before they come to dinner, and I feel that is a good idea – saves that last minute panic if an old friend has suddenly switched from rare steak and chips to a Pritikin-style diet!

This meal should not offend too many guests and I feel certain that those who eat it will find it enjoyable, and will not feel too guilty about having committed dietary sins.

AVOCADO WITH MARINATED
VEGETABLES AND TARRAGON DRESSING

SPIRITED CHICKEN

MEDLEY OF WILD AND BROWN RICES
WITH MUSHROOMS OF FIELD AND
FOREST

TOSSED GREEN SALAD*

RASPBERRY BAVARIAN MOULD WITH
FRESH BERRIES

AVOCADO WITH MARINATED VEGETABLES

Serves 4

1 medium green capsicum, seeded and thinly sliced
1 medium tomato, chopped
2 medium spring onions, sliced
6 large green beans, lightly cooked and cut into thin strips
8 black olives, slivered
¾ cup Tarragon Dressing
2 medium avocados, stoned and halved
4 large red-leaf lettuce leaves

Combine capsicum, tomato, spring onions, beans and olives in a shallow dish and marinate in Tarragon Dressing at room temperature for 30 minutes.

Arrange avocado halves on lettuce leaves and surround with vegetables. Add 1 teaspoon of Tarragon Dressing to each avocado and serve, passing the remaining dressing separately.

TARRAGON DRESSING

Makes ¾ cup

4 tbsp extra-light olive oil
1 tbsp cider vinegar
2 tsp fresh orange juice
1 tsp fresh chopped tarragon or ½ tsp dried tarragon
seasoned pepper

Combine all ingredients in jar with tight fitting lid and shake well. Chill until ready to serve. Cover and chill unused portion.

SPIRITED CHICKEN

A flambé dish always adds a sense of 'occasion' to a meal. Flaming the brandy evaporates the alcohol, leaving behind only the superb flavour.

4 whole chicken breasts
1 tsp fresh chopped dill
1 tsp fresh thyme leaves
½ tsp black pepper
1 tbsp butter or olive oil
2 cloves garlic, crushed or finely chopped
3 tbsp brandy
1 tsp Worcestershire sauce
2 tbsp cream
60g ham, finely shredded
4 spring onions, finely chopped

Remove skin from chicken and carefully remove chicken meat from bones, giving 8 individual fillets; flatten slightly.

Coat chicken breasts with combined herbs and pepper. Heat butter in saucepan, add garlic and chicken and sauté until golden brown and cooked through, about 10 minutes.

Add warmed brandy and set aflame. When flames die down, remove chicken from pan and keep warm. Add to the pan, Worcestershire sauce, cream, ham and spring onions. Stir until sauce just boils. Spoon sauce over chicken and serve at once.

MEDLEY OF WILD AND BROWN RICES WITH MUSHROOMS OF FIELD AND FOREST

Serves 4

Because this is a dinner party, I have added the extravagant touch of using wild rice and dried morels. However, the cost can be reduced by using all brown rice or even substituting the black, sticky Chinese rice for wild rice. To use the Chinese rice, cook it only until the grains are tender but will still separate easily, rather than cooking it until the texture is claggy – the way it is traditionally served. Ordinary field mushrooms or a mixture of these with oyster mushrooms and Chinese-dried mushrooms offers an interesting but more economical alternative.

¾ cup wild rice
2 cups water
½ cup brown rice
30g dried morels, porcini or other dried mushrooms
3 large French shallots or 1 small white onion, thickly sliced
6 large spring onions
250g small fresh mushrooms, halved
1 tbsp butter or light olive oil
freshly ground pepper
⅓–⅔ cup chicken stock (see p 133)

Cook wild rice in a large amount of boiling water until just tender, about 35 minutes. Drain well. Combine 1 cup of water and brown rice in heavy saucepan; bring to the boil, reduce heat to low, cover and cook until water is absorbed, about 35 minutes.

Meanwhile, soak dried mushrooms in sufficient hot water to cover, for 30 minutes. Drain. Cut morels in half if large, rinse well, squeeze dry and cut off any woody stems. Slice shallots thickly and chop spring onions.

Melt butter in heavy 25 cm pan over high heat. Add shallots and stir 1 minute. Add all mushrooms and cook until juices are just beginning to run, stirring frequently, about 4 minutes. Add wild and brown rice and pepper and cook until mixture is almost dry, stirring often, about 4 minutes. Mix in ⅓ cup stock and cook until just warmed through, stirring occasionally. Stir in spring onions. If dry, add remaining ⅓ cup stock. Adjust seasonings. Serve very hot.

RASPBERRY BAVARIAN MOULD WITH FRESH BERRIES

Serves 8

If raspberries are out of season, strawberries may be substituted. Another alternative is to use dried apricots which have been soaked overnight and well drained.

1½ flat tbsp gelatine (or 1½ sheets gelatine)
¼ cup hot water
1 cup milk
1 cup buttermilk
2 eggs, separated
½ cup castor sugar
1 tsp lemon juice
1½ cups sweet, ripe raspberries, crushed
½ cup light cream, whipped
additional fresh berries
mint or strawberry leaves for garnish

Soften gelatine in the hot water. Scald milk and remove from heat; add gelatine and stir until dissolved. Add the buttermilk and stir in.

Lightly beat egg yolks and stir together with the sugar. Gradually add the hot milk and beat well. Place basin over simmering water and cook until the custard coats a wooden spoon. Remove from heat and chill until mixture begins to set. Add the lemon juice and crushed raspberries and stir well. Beat egg whites until stiff, whip the cream and combine the two. Fold into the first mixture, mixing lightly but thoroughly. Pour into a wetted mould or into a loaf tin and chill until set.

Cut into slices or wedges and serve with fresh berries.

If desired, make a coulis of fresh raspberries or strawberries and add a dash of raspberry eau de vie or liqueur.

A SELECTION OF AFTERNOON TEA TREATS

Now unless you can be sure that your family or guests will be able to resist sampling each of the treats that follow, I don't suggest you serve all these at the one time. Although each of these recipes is acceptable when eaten individually, it would certainly overstep the boundaries of 'almost healthy' eating to sample a piece of each!

Mix and match these with other snacks which are low in fats or sugars and just offer one or two of these treats as just that – a treat and an indulgence.

FRESH FIG AND WALNUT CAKE

BUTTERMILK SCONES

LEANNE'S SPONGE

STRAWBERRY CHOCOLATE CUPS

LEMON TEA LOAF

FRESH FIG AND WALNUT CAKE

Makes about 10 wedges

Fresh figs, lemon peel and walnuts combine to offer a splendid flavour in this moist cake. Very good as an afternoon tea or luncheon cake. I have to tell those of my readers who are unrepentant 'dietary sinners' that it makes a wonderful dessert cake served warm with ice cream or cream!!

1½ cups chopped ripe figs
½ cup finely chopped walnuts
⅔ cup raw sugar
2 tbsp processed bran
2 tsp lemon juice
1 tsp Grand Marnier
finely grated rind of 1 lemon
125g butter, dairy spread or margarine
2 eggs
1¼ cups plain wholemeal flour
1½ tsp baking powder
½ cup unflavoured yoghurt

Combine chopped figs, walnuts, ⅓ cup sugar, bran, cinnamon, lemon juice and rind in a bowl and toss together.

Using a large bowl, cream together remaining sugar and the butter. Add eggs one at a time, beating well after each addition. Mix together flour and baking powder. Alternating with the yoghurt, stir other dry ingredients into the creamed mixture, mixing lightly but thoroughly.

Lightly butter and dust with flour a deep sponge tin. Spoon in half the cake batter and spread evenly. Spoon on half the fig mixture and spread to the edges.

Gently spoon on and spread remainder of cake batter and top with the rest of the fig and nut mixture, spread to the edges.

Place on centre shelf in a preheated 180°C oven and bake for 50 minutes, or until cake is barely firm to the touch.

Cool in tin before storing in a well sealed cake tin.

BUTTERMILK SCONES

Makes 10–12

Scones are among the most versatile of afternoon tea snacks – and they have the great advantage of cooking in about 12 minutes. Many a time have I been stricken to see guests coming up the path (and you must understand that food writers can never serve bought biscuits or cakes!) and have been saved by baking a quick batch of scones to serve with homemade jam.

I always use cream-of-tartar self-raising flour; not only do the scones rise better, but they never have the slightly raspy aftertaste which phosphate rising agents can produce. Although the buttermilk gives these scones a nice tang and a light texture, for results that are almost as good use the same recipe with ordinary milk or half milk and water.

2 cups cream-of-tartar self-raising flour
1 tsp butter (optional)
about ⅔ cup cultured buttermilk (or milk soured with a little lemon or vinegar)

Sift the flour into a basin. (Scones and sponges are about the only recipes for which I sift flour, I must admit.) Lightly rub in the butter, lifting the floury mixture in the fingers well above the bowl and allowing it to drop back in – this adds air to the mixture. Make a well in the centre and pour in the buttermilk. Mix with the blade of a knife – another 'old cook's trick' to add lightness.

Mix only until dough holds together, tip onto a board and very lightly pat into a rough rectangle. (**Never, never** roll them – I am sometimes horrified by having work experience students from home economics colleges do this.) Using a metal scone cutter or a knife, cut the dough into 12 portions. Place these onto a lightly floured baking tray and place into a preheated 250°C oven on a middle shelf, and bake for 10–12 minutes.

Remove from oven, wrap in a tea-towel to cool. Serve with a little butter and jam, preferably homemade.

Excellent herb scones may be made from the same recipe. To do this, I put 1 cup of the flour into the food processor with about 1 tablespoon roughly chopped herbs and whirr them until the herbs are very finely chopped and the flour has a delicate green tint. I then proceed as above.

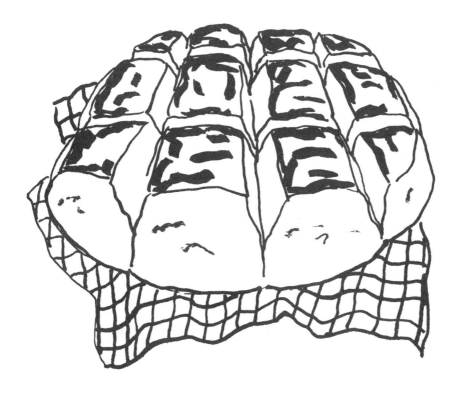

LEANNE'S SPONGE

Makes 1 large double and 1 small single

A beautiful sponge – not too sinful in itself, so it depends upon the cook's choice of filling and topping. I suggest a little cream with a topping of passionfruit and strawberries. Bliss indeed and worth the sacrifice of other fattening foods!

1 cup cornflour
1 tsp baking powder
¾ tsp bicarbonate of soda
5 eggs, separated
¾ cup castor sugar
cream
strawberries
passionfruit

Sift the bicarbonate of soda and baking powder with the cornflour twice.

Beat the egg white until stiff, add the sugar and beat until dissolved and glossy, about 5 minutes. Add egg yolks and beat in. Sift in dry ingredients (this constitutes the third sifting) and fold through, gently but thoroughly.

Pour mixture into buttered and floured tins and bake in a preheated 180°C oven for 25–30 minutes.

STRAWBERRY CHOCOLATE CUPS

Makes 24

These delectable morsels cannot even pretend to be 'almost healthy', but they are delicious, and may be served with coffee instead of dessert.

I have made them with carob, and filled them with a whipped cottage cheese very lightly flavoured with a drop of Grand Marnier, and they do become more acceptably healthy that way.

200g dark eating chocolate
6 tbsp whipped reduced cream or whipped light cream
cheese
24 strawberries, washed, hulled and halved
24 confectionary-sized paper patty cases

Half fill electric frypan with water and turn onto low heat. Place chocolate in a jar or bowl and place into frypan to melt chocolate, being careful not to let the water steam too much as this affects both the colour and texture of the chocolate.

When chocolate is melted, place a teaspoonful into each patty pan and, using a small brush, spread the chocolate over the base and up the sides of the cases. Chill until chocolate sets.

To serve, spoon a teaspoon of whipped cream into each, arrange 2 strawberry halves on top and granish with a small mint leaf.

A delicious addition is to splash a little of your favourite liqueur into the base of the chocolate case before spooning in the cream or alternately the strawberries may be marinated in the liqueur.

LEMON TEA LOAF

Makes 1 loaf

½ cup butter, softened
¾ cup castor sugar
2 eggs
1½ cups plain flour
1½ tsp baking powder
½ cup milk
½ cup chopped walnuts
3 tbsp finely grated lemon rind

Preheat oven to 180°C. Butter and flour a 30 × 9 × 5 cm loaf tin.

Using an electric mixer, cream butter and sugar in a large bowl. Beat in eggs one at a time. Sift in flour and baking powder and beat at low speed until smooth. Blend in milk. Fold in walnuts and lemon peel. Pour batter into prepared tin and bake in preheated 180°C oven for 40 minutes.

Cool tin on wire rack for 10 minutes. Invert loaf onto rack and cool completely before serving.

Opposite: A Sturdy Meal, see page 56
Overleaf left: An Italian Dinner, see page 61
Overleaf right: A Little Lunch for Six, see page 67
Opposite page 91: A Touch of the Middle East, see page 72

A SIMPLE COUNTRY REPAST

This meal is similar to several I ate when I was travelling around France. I travelled by train and stayed at lots of tiny country hotels. Perhaps I was lucky, but the food was always excellent and I enjoyed a particular chicken dish which reminded me of one my grandmother served at home. I remember too the vividly salmon-pink quinces I ate in Normandy on a lovely autumn day. I have never achieved quite that same perfection in my stewed quinces, but I keep trying! The ones I savoured were served with wickedly thick Normandy cream, but for 'almost healthy' eaters I suggest yoghurt or a light, whipped cream as a substitute.

VEGETABLE AND OATMEAL SOUP

POACHED CHICKEN WITH VEGETABLES

GREEN VEGETABLE*

SIMMERED QUINCES

VEGETABLE AND OATMEAL SOUP

Serves 6

My Nanna, a Scot, used oatmeal extensively in her cooking. This is one of the soups I remember fondly from my childhood. Easily made, it is still one of the most delicious I have had.

1½lt well flavoured chicken, veal or lamb stock,
*   completely free of fat*
2 carrots, coarsely chopped
2 parsnips, coarsely chopped
1 small turnip, coarsely chopped
2 sticks celery with leaves, coarsely chopped
2 white onions, chopped
little salt (optional)
black pepper
⅓ cup oatmeal
chopped parsley

Combine all ingredients, except oatmeal, in a large saucepan. Bring to the boil, reduce heat and simmer for at least 1½ hours, at which stage vegetables will be very tender and the flavour mellow. Add the oatmeal and continue cooking for another 20 minutes. Add parsley. Serve in heated bowls with bread or toast.

This soup freezes well in thoroughly washed milk cartons.

POACHED CHICKEN WITH VEGETABLES

Serves 6

A few years ago it was very trendy to cook and serve a whole chicken in a terracotta chicken brick. Fashion is fickle and one seldom sees these cooking utensils nowadays. However, they did cook well and I still use mine to cook this particular dish. If you don't have a 'chicken brick' – I think that is what they were called – use a casserole with a well fitted lid and you will enjoy a similar result.

1 large roasting chicken, preferably free range
3 carrots
3 parsnips
2 sprigs fresh thyme or ¾ teaspoon dried thyme
1 cup chicken stock
1 cup dry white wine
plenty of pepper
parsley sprigs

Carefully remove all skin from the chicken and any fat from within the bird's cavity. Discard. Place the chicken into the chicken brick or a small casserole. Scrub or peel carrots and parsnips and cut into four lengthwise. Arrange beside the chicken.

Place the herb sprigs on the chicken. Pour over the stock and white wine and sprinkle with pepper. Cover the chicken tightly and cook for about 1¼ hours in a moderately low oven. Skim off any fat which rises to the surface.

To serve, cut chicken into portions and place onto heated platters. Serve a portion of the vegetables with each and spoon over some of the broth. It is best to serve this dish in large, shallow soup bowls if you have them. Serve with rice or noodles and with plenty of good bread to mop up the delectable juices.

A simple French salad goes well with this dish – one of the very best when it is well prepared.

SIMMERED QUINCES

Serves 6

4 large quinces, peeled, cored and cut into thick slices
water to cover
1/2 cup honey
1/2 cinnamon stick
piece of vanilla bean or 1/2 tsp vanilla essence

Place quince slices into a heavy saucepan, add the water, honey, piece of cinnamon stick and vanilla bean (if using). Cover and cook **very gently** for at least 1 hour, or until quince slices are tender and prettily pink. Add vanilla essence if using instead of a bean.

Set aside to cool, but do not chill.

Serve with yoghurt or a little whipped light cream. Sour cream at 18 per cent butterfat content is a pleasant and acceptable accompaniment.

A SPECIAL OCCASION MENU

Not a difficult menu, but it does look a bit special to serve quail eggs and a roulade, which seems to intimidate some cooks. This is a very easy, failproof one, but don't admit to that. Chocolate mousse seems to be a universal favourite, but this one is more acceptable than most in an 'almost healthy' eating programme.

SCOTCH QUAIL EGGS

SPINACH ROULADE

SNOW PEA SALAD WITH WALNUT VINAIGRETTE

NAUGHTY BUT NICE CHOCOLATE MOUSSE

SCOTCH QUAIL EGGS

Serves 6 as a first course

12 quail eggs*
500 g chicken flesh
2 tbsp chopped parsley
1 tsp very finely chopped green ginger root
1 tsp very finely grated lemon rind
little salt and pepper
little flour
watercress

Place quail eggs into a small saucepan of cold water; bring to the boil, reduce heat slightly and cook 2–3 minutes. Remove eggs from the water, crack shells and place eggs into cold water. When cool enough to handle, remove the shells. Meanwhile, finely mince the chicken meat. Add the green ginger, lemon rind and pepper to the meat and work in thoroughly.

When eggs are cold, divide the meat mixture into 12 portions and shape one portion neatly around each egg. Lightly flour each covered egg, arrange eggs on a lightly buttered oven tray and bake in a preheated moderate oven at 180°C for about 20 minutes.

Eggs may be served moderately hot, or cold. To serve, cut eggs lengthwise and arrange on small platters in a nest of watercress sprigs. Serve with Lemon Mayonnaise (see recipe p 17).

A deliciously different addition to a picnic basket.

*If you don't want to use quail eggs, substitute one small hen egg for 2 quail eggs.

SPINACH ROULADE

Serves 6–8

PANCAKE

2 tsp unsalted butter, melted
1 cup sifted plain flour
1 tsp baking powder
2 cups low fat milk
2 eggs

FILLING

2 tsp melted butter
1 clove garlic, finely chopped
½ cup almonds, chopped
½ cup spring onions, chopped
350g well drained cooked spinach, chopped finely
½ cup lean ham, finely chopped
1½ cups grated tasty cheese
¼ tsp thyme
¼ tsp ground nutmeg
¼ tsp seasoned pepper

Preheat oven to 190°C. Brush melted butter over Swiss roll tin 25 × 37 cm.

Sift flour and baking powder together. Using electric mixer beat in eggs and milk until smooth. Pour batter into prepared pan and bake until barely brown, about 20–25 minutes.

Filling Melt butter in a medium-sized pan over moderately high heat. Add garlic, cook lightly and add ham. Add spring onions and almonds and cook until lightly browned. Stir in flour, thyme, nutmeg and pepper and cook for 1 minute. Add spinach and heat through, stirring constantly. Remove from heat and set aside.

Remove pancake from oven and turn onto a damp tea-towel, keeping flat. Allow to cool slightly. Spread filling over pancake, leaving edges of base free of mixture. Sprinkle cheese over top.

Carefully roll up lengthwise and allow to stand for 10 minutes. Cut into 6 or 8 portions and serve.

SNOW PEA SALAD WITH WALNUT VINAIGRETTE

Serves 6

500g fresh snow peas, strings removed
1½ tbsp fresh lime juice or lemon juice
2 tsp light salt soy sauce
¼ cup walnut oil
3 thin spring onions, sliced thinly on the diagonal
2 tsp minced fresh ginger root

Blanch the snow peas in boiling water until bright green, 45–60 seconds. Drain and refresh under cold running water; drain well and pat dry. Place peas into serving bowl.

In a small bowl, whisk the lime juice and soy sauce until well blended. Whisk in the walnut oil and stir in the spring onions and ginger. Pour vinaigrette over the snow peas and toss until well coated.

NAUGHTY BUT NICE CHOCOLATE MOUSSE

Serves 6

Actually this isn't too wicked when the ingredients are divided by six! Because it has a dense texture, it is quite rich and a small portion is satisfying.

I used to include this in my dieters' weight loss programme and they loved it – but still lost weight!

125g dark chocolate
1 tbsp strong black coffee
4 eggs, separated
3 tsp rum, brandy or a few drops vanilla essence

Break up chocolate and place into a basin with coffee. Melt over simmering, but not boiling, water, stirring until smooth.

Remove from heat and stir in egg yolks one at a time, stirring until well blended.

Beat egg whites stiffly and stir or fold very gently into chocolate mixture, together with flavouring. Spoon into small mousse pots and refrigerate for several hours or overnight. Garnish with a fresh flower or herb leaf.

AN ENTERTAINING MENU

This involves a little more trouble than some of the other menus, but it is most enjoyable. The first course pasta is delicious, and may be served as a main course on other occasions. The flavours of the main dish are piquant, the tartness of the apples and the crème fraîche adding a tang. If preferred, you may substitute plain yoghurt for the higher fat content of the crème fraîche. If you feel the dessert soufflé is too rich, substitute chilled orange segments sprinkled with mint or orange liqueur. Remember that the individual dishes which make up our menus may be swapped for others which you prefer or which you feel would give a better balance to the meal you are planning to serve.

WHOLEMEAL PASTA WITH TOASTED
HAZELNUT SAUCE

SAUTEED CHICKEN WITH CIDER AND
APPLES

GREEN VEGETABLE*

BABY NEW POTATOES WITH PARSLEY*

BRANDIED ORANGE SOUFFLES

WHOLEMEAL PASTA WITH TOASTED HAZELNUT SAUCE

Serves 4 as an entrée

Pasta is acknowledged as being a desirable high
fibre element in what we regard now as a healthy
eating programme. Homemade or commercial
pasta may be used; remember that fresh pasta
takes only minutes to cook.

The hazelnuts offer an interesting flavour –
they are being grown now by Australian nut
farmers and are delicious as an ingredient.

1 tbsp extra-light olive oil
¾ cup coarsely chopped lightly toasted hazelnuts
1 clove garlic, very finely chopped
about 4 tbsp finely chopped fresh parsley
coarsely ground pepper
250g wholemeal fettucine
½ cup rich chicken stock
2 tbsp light cream
1 tbsp finely chopped mixed herbs (such as French
  tarragon, basil, marjoram)
pepper
finely grated Parmigiana cheese (optional)

Place shelled hazelnuts onto a tray and toast in a moderate –
low oven until the skin of nuts begin to peel. Peel off as much
skin as possible, either by rubbing the toasted hazelnuts
between the hands or in a tea-towel. Chop coarsely.

Heat the oil, add the nuts and cook until deep gold, stirring
often.

Add garlic, parsley and a little salt (if using) and pepper.
Cook the pasta in a large pot of rapidly boiling water.
Combine chicken stock and cream in a small saucepan, add
herbs and pepper and simmer gently for about 5 minutes.
Drain cooked pasta well, pour on sauce and sprinkle with the
toasted hazelnuts.

Serve grated cheese separately if using.

SAUTEED CHICKEN WITH CIDER AND APPLES

Serves 4–5

1.5 kg chicken, cut into portions
2 tbsp butter or butter and oil
3 tbsp chopped spring onions
1 cup dry apple cider
2 sage leaves or good pinch dried sage
½ cup rich chicken stock
2 cups peeled and sliced Granny Smith apples
¼ cup crème fraîche

Remove all skin from chicken pieces. Heat butter in a heavy pan and cook chicken until golden brown, approximately 15 minutes, turning from time to time with tongs. Remove to a platter and keep warm.

Chop onions, add to pan and sauté. Pour in cider and chicken stock, add sage and return chicken pieces to pan and cover. Simmer until tender, about 25–30 minutes.

In a heavy saucepan, gently poach apple slices in a little water or additional cider for about 10 minutes, turning slices several times during cooking time. Set aside and keep hot.

Skim all fat from chicken pan juices and reduce over high heat for 5 minutes; stir in the crème fraîche and reduce sauce for 2–3 minutes, or until slightly thickened. Return chicken to pan and simmer over gentle heat, basting with sauce. Arrange chicken on a platter, spoon on apple slices and sauce, and serve.

BRANDIED ORANGE SOUFFLES

Serves 4

3 tbsp butter or substitute
4 tbsp plain flour
¼ cup sugar
½ cup milk
½ cup orange juice
2 tbsp brandy or Grand Marnier
4 eggs, separated

Melt butter in the top of a double saucepan over simmering water. Add flour and stir until smooth. Add sugar, milk and orange juice and continue stirring over simmering water until sauce thickens. Remove from heat, cool and add brandy or Grand Marnier.

Beat egg yolks until pale and fluffy and fold into orange mixture. Beat the egg whites until soft peaks form, then fold into soufflé mixture. Pour mixture into 4 small greased individual soufflé dishes and bake in a moderate oven for 20–25 minutes, or until golden brown. Serve dusted with icing sugar and topped with a strawberry.

A CASUAL MEAL FOR FOUR

This is for one of those casual occasions when it seems a good idea to invite a couple of friends over for an informal meal.

Start with a tasty dip and lots of vegetable sticks for dipping – offer some torn, warmed pita bread as well if you feel the need for something a little more substantial.

The meatballs are delicious and the poached pears offer a fragrant conclusion to an enjoyable meal.

SMOKED OYSTER AND TUNA DIP WITH VEGETABLE BATONS

MIDDLE EASTERN MEATBALLS WITH CORIANDER FLAVOURED SAUCE

LEBANESE SALAD

POACHED PEARS WITH GINGER AND PISTACHIOS

SMOKED OYSTER AND TUNA DIP

Serves 4

1 can smoked oysters, well drained
1 small can tuna in brine, well drained
1 spring onion, chopped
125 g cottage cheese
2 tbsp coarsely chopped parsley
black pepper
lemon juice to taste

Place all ingredients into a food processor and chop coarsely. Spoon into a bowl and mix well. Chill slightly.

Serve with carrot sticks, celery slices, red capsicum slices, cucumber slices etc. Also serve pieces of warm pita bread if desired.

LEBANESE SALAD

Serves 4

4 ripe tomatoes, chopped
2 small white onions, chopped or 6 spring onions,
   finely chopped
1 Continental cucumber, chopped or 4 small Lebanese
   cucumbers, thinly sliced
⅓ cup chopped parsley
pepper

Chop the tomatoes, onion and cucumber and arrange in layers in a bowl.

Top with the parsley and sprinkle on the pepper. Allow to stand for several hours, then toss together. A little lemon juice may be added if desired.

MIDDLE EASTERN MEATBALLS WITH CORIANDER FLAVOURED SAUCE

Makes 24 small meatballs; serves 4

SAUCE

¾ cup unflavoured thick yoghurt
½ cup finely chopped fresh coriander
½ tsp cumin
squeeze of lemon juice

MEATBALLS

¼ cup sultanas
2 tbsp finely chopped spring onions
⅓ cup lightly toasted pinenuts
½ tsp cumin
½ tsp ground cinnamon
½ tsp ground allspice
1 clove garlic, finely chopped
little salt (optional)
freshly ground pepper
250g minced lean lamb
3 tbsp extra-light olive oil

To make sauce, mix together yoghurt, coriander, cumin and lemon juice. Set aside while preparing meatballs.

To make meatballs, soak sultanas in a little boiling water for 10 minutes, then drain well and chop. Combine sultanas, spring onions, pine nuts, cumin, allspice, garlic, salt (if using) and pepper in a bowl and mix. Add the minced lamb and knead in until well blended. Form into 24 balls.

Heat olive oil in a large heavy frying pan until hot, but not smoking. Cook the meatballs for a few minutes, turning each several times. Drain well on kitchen paper and serve with the dipping sauce.

A Stylish Dinner Party, see page 78

POACHED PEARS WITH GINGER AND PISTACHIOS

Serves 4

This is a fragrant and delicious dessert which may be prepared a day in advance. If you really can't stand ginger, substitute a little glacé citrus peel instead.

2 large pears, peeled
2 tbsp honey
1½ cups water
piece of orange peel
piece of lemon peel
2 cloves
30g chopped glacé ginger
30g skinned and coarsely chopped pistachio nuts
little shredded orange peel
unflavoured yoghurt or crème fraîche

Peel pears, cut in halves and remove cores; place into a saucepan with the honey, water, orange and lemon peel and cloves. Poach gently until pears are tender. Remove pears with a slotted spoon, and discard peel and cloves. Chill the pears. Boil liquid until it reduces by one-third.

Place the chilled pear halves onto serving platters. Spoon a small portion of the mixed ginger and pistachio nuts into the hollow of each and spoon on a portion of the syrup. Garnish with orange shreds. Serve with a spoonful of yoghurt or crème fraîche.

A Selection of Afternoon Tea Treats, see page 84

A VERSATILE DINNER MENU

This is a lovely menu to serve at any time of the year. A warm or cold first course, followed by a substantial main course, with a refreshingly light dessert to finish the meal provides a good balance and ensures that guests will leave the table feeling replete but comfortable – an important point in 'almost healthy' eating.

CHILLED OR WARM CHICKEN AND AVOCADO SOUP

ROSEMARY RACKS OF LAMB

GOURMET POTATOES

BABY GREEN BEANS*

LEMON WATER ICE

CHILLED CHICKEN AND AVOCADO SOUP

Serves 6

The success of this recipe depends upon the depth of flavour in the chicken stock. To ensure this richness, follow my recipe on page 133. To avoid discoloration, add the avocado at the last minute before serving.

6 cups rich chicken stock, well chilled
2 small, ripe avocados
1 spring onion, finely chopped
½ cup dry white wine
⅓ cup light cream or well stirred yoghurt
black pepper
wafer thin slices of avocado and unpeeled cucumber

Combine chicken stock, chopped avocados, spring onion and white wine and mix together. Put through a food processor or blender in batches and purée until quite smooth. Pour into small chilled bowls, and stir a little of the cream into each. Garnish with wafer thin slices of avocado and cucumber and serve at once.

If preferred, soup may be served warm, but do not allow it to boil – this causes the avocados to become bitter. Replace garnish of vegetable slices with wholemeal croutons or finely chopped spring onion greens.

ROSEMARY RACKS OF LAMB

Serves 6

racks of lamb (allow 2–3 cutlets per person)
2 tbsp light olive oil
1/3 cup lemon juice
2 cloves garlic, finely chopped
2 tbsp flour
1/3 cup white wine
1/3 cup dry vermouth
1/2 cup water
1 tbsp honey
2 tsp lemon rind
2 tbsp fresh rosemary, very finely chopped
pepper
1/4 cup fresh mint leaves or rosemary sprigs

Trim every scrap of fat from the lamb cutlets; place cutlets in a bowl with combined oil and lemon juice, add garlic and leave to marinate for a few hours, turning several times during marination. When ready to cook lamb, place racks with the marinade into a roasting pan and cook at 180°C for about 30 minutes or until cooked. Remove from oven, strain pan juices and reserve.

Return lamb to barely warm oven while preparing sauce.

Pour 1/4 cup pan juices into a saucepan and blend in the flour; stir until combined and cook, stirring, for a few seconds. Add rosemary, pan juices, wine, vermouth, water and honey and stir until the sauce boils and thickens. Reduce heat, add lemon rind and chopped rosemary and season with pepper. Remove lamb from oven, slice into cutlets and arrange on a serving platter. Spoon sauce over the cutlets and garnish with fresh rosemary sprigs and mint leaves.

GOURMET POTATOES

Serves 6

A healthy alternative to the delicious, but fattening, Potatoes Anna.

3 onions, finely sliced
½ cup finely chopped parsley
2 cups shredded spinach or silver beet
500g potatoes, thinly sliced
freshly ground pepper
1¼ cups chicken stock
2 tbsp grated tasty cheese

Using an ovenproof dish, spoon in a layer of chopped onions, next spread a layer of combined parsley and silverbeet, then top with a layer of potatoes; add a sprinkling of pepper. Repeat layers of vegetables; add more pepper. Pour over chicken stock and sprinkle cheese over the top.

Bake in a moderately hot oven for about 45 minutes, testing from time to time to see when potatoes are tender.

Serve as a vegetable.

LEMON WATER ICE

Serves 6

It is of course the sugar which is the 'dubious' ingredient in this recipe, but a small portion of this tangy treat is acceptable once in a while.

¾ cup granulated sugar
2 cups cold water
½ cup lemon juice
2 tsp grated lemon rind
1 egg white
1 tbsp castor sugar
julienned lemon peel shreds in syrup

Combine sugar and water in a saucepan; mix together. Stir over low heat until sugar dissolves. Stir in lemon juice and rind, then allow to cool. Strain liquid into a freezer tray and freeze until mushy, stirring from time to time. Spoon into a bowl.

Beat egg white until stiff and gradually beat in the sugar to make a meringue.

Fold this into lemon mixture, return to tray and freeze. (But not too solidly.)

Serve in scoops, topped with lemon peel shreds and fresh herb leaves or tiny flowers.

LEMON PEEL SHREDS

1 cup water
1 cup sugar
finely shredded peel of 2–3 lemons

Combine sugar and water in a saucepan, heating slowly until dissolved. Stir well. Add the peel, reduce heat and allow to simmer very gently until lemon shreds are transparent.

Store in refrigerator in the syrup and use a few drained shreds as required.

Orange peel may be prepared in the same way.

A PERSONAL INDULGENCE

I guess most people who work with food are often asked their own preferences – I know I am. Perhaps the most often asked question is: 'What would be your favourite meal?' And the answer is embarrassingly simple ... I don't ask for complex sauces or exotic ingredients, and it certainly is 'almost healthy', so I am prepared to share it with you. Of course, it does vary a bit from season to season, but, assuming it is springtime and the asparagus is rising, this would be my own choice.

BABY ASPARAGUS WITH LEMON JUICE
AND PEPPER

GRILLED TROUT

BABY NEW POTATOES WITH PEPPER*

GREEN SALAD WITH FRENCH DRESSING*

FRESH FRUIT SALAD WITH A LITTLE
CREAM

DRY WHITE WINE (Preferably FUME
BLANC)*

BABY ASPARAGUS WITH LEMON JUICE AND PEPPER

As I write this, asparagus is well out of season but my mouth waters at the thought.

250g asparagus, trimmed
juice of half a lemon
seasoned pepper

Bring lightly salted water to the boil, plunge in the asparagus which has been snapped off at the base and peeled just a little.

Cook for about 10 minutes, remove and drain well. Squeeze on lemon juice, sprinkle generously with pepper and eat with the fingers!

GRILLED TROUT

1 serving

1 trout
2 tsp butter, melted
pepper
lemon juice

Wipe the fish and pat dry if necessary. Brush each side with a little melted butter, place under a preheated griller and cook for 6 minutes each side, turning halfway through cooking time. Place onto a platter and sprinkle with lemon juice and pepper.

To eat with the least difficulty, cut along the side of the fish, where there is a clearly defined line. Using the fork, peel back the flesh. When top side has been eaten, either turn over the fish or remove backbone and eat the underside.

Serve with a simple green salad tossed with a little French dressing, a good French-style bread stick, and, of course, those little new potatoes.

FRESH FRUIT SALAD

Serves 1

This is the simple fruit salad of my childhood and I still find it absolutely delicious. For me, a 'real' fruit salad must have all these ingredients – they provide the right combination of texture and flavours.

1 or 2 slices fresh pineapple (when desperate, I have
*   been known to use unsweetened canned pineapple)*
1 red apple, unpeeled and coarsely chopped
1 orange, peeled and segmented
1 banana, sliced
½ cup orange juice
1 or 2 passionfruit
about ½ tsp sugar

Cut the pineapple into chunks and combine with all the other ingredients. Cover and chill for 1 hour. Serve with a spoonful of cream.

If you have other fruits such as plums, strawberries, peaches etc., these may be added to the fruit salad, but the ingredients listed above are the vital ones!

A VEGETARIAN DINNER

This could be served either as a family meal or as a menu for guests. The main course is substantial, so serve a light first course with plenty of crunchy vegetable crudites. There are anchovies in the salad, but, for vegetarians, these are eliminated. Substitute a little soy sauce to add the tang of salt the salad needs. Serve fresh fruits of your choice for dessert or a simple dessert of baked or puréed apples.

To serve the dip, place onto the table with the crudites.

CURRY CREAM DIP

ASSORTED VEGETABLE CRUDITES*

WALNUT CHEESE BALLS WITH CHEESE SAUCE

GREEN SALAD* WITH MUSTARD YOGHURT DRESSING

CAULIFLOWER SALAD

FRESH FRUITS*

CURRY CREAM DIP

250g cottage cheese, chopped
2 tsp sweet mango chutney
2 tsp mayonnaise
15g green ginger root, peeled and finely grated
½ spring onion, chopped finely
1½ tsp mild curry paste
squeeze of lemon juice
grated rind of ½ lemon

In a large bowl, combine cream cheese, chutney, mayonnaise, ginger root, spring onion, curry paste, lemon juice and rind. Beat until smooth and well blended and spoon into small bowls to serve. Accompany with a variety of vegetable crudites.

WALNUT CHEESE BALLS

Serves 6

A splendid dish to serve a vegetarian guest!
Nutritious as well as delicious.

½ white onion, finely chopped or grated
little olive oil
125g tasty cheese, grated
185g walnuts
2 slices wholemeal bread, crusts removed
⅓ cup finely chopped parsley
150ml skim milk
2 tbsp wheatgerm
2 eggs
pepper
600ml Cheese Sauce
additional chopped parsley

Heat a little olive oil and sauté onions. Combine walnuts, bread and parsley in blender or processor and mix to a fine consistency.

Combine onion, cheese, walnuts, breadcrumbs and parsley in a large bowl. Add milk, wheatgerm and pepper. Beat eggs and stir into mixture. With lightly floured hands, roll mixture into golf ball-sized rounds and arrange in a shallow buttered oven dish. Make up cheese sauce and pour over the walnut cheese balls. Makes about 20 balls. Bake in a moderately hot oven at 190°C for 35 minutes. Serve very hot, sprinkled with chopped parsley. For meat eaters, a little grilled, crumbled bacon may be sprinkled over the dish just before serving.

Serve with green salad tossed with Mustard Yoghurt Dressing.

CHEESE SAUCE

3 tbsp butter or margarine
½ white onion, finely chopped
3 tbsp wholemeal flour
600ml reduced fat milk
1 tsp finely chopped fresh marjoram or ½ tsp dried marjoram
pepper
nutmeg
60g grated cheese

Heat butter or margarine in a saucepan and sauté onion until soft, but not coloured. Stir in the flour and cook for a couple of minutes, stirring constantly. Slowly pour in the warmed milk, whisking constantly. As the sauce thickens, add marjoram, pepper and nutmeg. Remove from heat and stir in grated cheese. Stir until melted.

Spoon over the walnut cheese balls and serve as directed.

MUSTARD YOGHURT DRESSING

This is a useful recipe if it is important to keep cholesterol levels low. It is not a mayonnaise but offers a tangy alternative.

3 tsp coarse-grained mustard
1½ tbsp light olive oil
¾ cup natural yoghurt
1 tbsp lemon juice
white pepper

Spoon mustard into a small mixing bowl, gradually add the olive oil and whisk vigorously. Add the yoghurt and blend in. Pour in the lemon juice, add pepper and whisk lightly. Cover and chill until required.

CAULIFLOWER SALAD

Serves 6–8

1 white cauliflower
2 anchovy fillets (for non-vegetarians)
8 stuffed olives, sliced
1 tbsp chopped capers, well rinsed and drained
1 tbsp finely chopped spring onions
3 tbsp olive oil
1 tbsp white wine vinegar
pepper

Wash and trim the cauliflower and break into florets. Cook in a small amount of boiling water to which a good squeeze of lemon juice has been added, for about 10 minutes or until tender crisp. Drain very thoroughly, cool and chill.

Soak anchovy fillets in a little milk for several hours, then drain and rinse well; pat dry and chop finely.

Place cauliflower florets, chopped fillets, olives, capers and spring onions into a bowl.

Shake together oil and vinegar, add pepper and pour over salad. Toss salad gently and serve at once.

A COMFORTABLE
WEEKEND MEAL

This meal can be put together easily and quickly and would be ideal for a holiday weekend away from home. Most of the preparation may be done in advance, always an advantage.

The main course looks most attractive, especially if green or autumn-tinted grape leaves are used to line serving plates.

For those who hesitate to indulge in champagne as part of the dessert – either from economy or concern for health – use a little orange juice topped up with plain soda water.

TANTALISING TASTE TEASERS WITH
VEGETABLE CRUDITES* AND RYE
ROUNDS*

POACHED CHICKEN, HAM AND GRAPE
SALAD

WHITE BEAN SALAD

MANGOES IN CHAMPAGNE

250g ricotta cheese, roughly chopped
2 tsp apricot brandy
1 stick celery, finely chopped
45g dried apricots, finely chopped
30g glacé ginger, finely chopped
1 tsp finely grated orange rind
¾ cup toasted sesame seeds

Beat the cheese with the brandy until softened. Add the chopped celery, apricots, ginger and orange rind. Chill mixture until firm; shape into marble-sized balls and roll lavishly in toasted sesame seeds.

Serve with vegetable crudites and rye bread rounds or Pecan Studded Rye Bread (see recipe p 9).

POACHED CHICKEN, HAM AND GRAPE SALAD

Serves 6–8

This is a wonderful salad for warm days, and it looks most inviting. Garnish the salad with grape leaves if they are available.

6–8 whole chicken breasts, skins removed and
  discarded
2 stalks celery with leaves, coarsely chopped
1 carrot, chopped
1 large onion, sliced
handful of parsley sprigs
1 bay leaf
1½ tsp curry paste or powder
few crushed peppercorns
1 lt water
salad greens of choice
250g lean cooked ham, cut into matchsticks
500g red and green grapes, rinsed and dried
extra small bunches of grapes

DRESSING

½ cup homemade mayonnaise
¼ cup plain yoghurt
¼ cup mango chutney, finely chopped or puréed
2 tsp lemon juice

Trim all vestiges of fat from the chicken and place into a saucepan with celery, onion, carrot, parsley, bay leaf, curry and peppercorns. Cover with water, bring to the boil and simmer for about 25 minutes or until tender. Drain chicken, remove bones, cut meat into cubes and chill.

Arrange washed and chilled greens on a platter. Combine chicken, ham, stemmed grapes and dressing and toss gently to mix. Serve at once, garnished with grape leaves and small grape bunches.

To make dressing, combine all ingredients and mix well.

WHITE BEAN SALAD

1½ cups lima or preferred dried white beans
1 onion, thinly sliced
2 cloves garlic, well crushed
freshly ground black pepper
2 tbsp light olive oil
6 spring onions (including greens), chopped
1 tbsp white wine vinegar
2 tsp lemon juice
black pepper
chopped parsley

Soak beans overnight in lightly salted water. Drain next day and discard water (which can help cause the flatulence sometimes caused by eating dried beans). Place beans into a saucepan, cover with cold water and gently cook for about 2 hours or until tender. Drain well.

Place the sliced onion and garlic into a large bowl and pour on the oil. Allow to stand for at least 1 hour. Add well drained beans, chopped spring onions, pepper and parsley. Sprinkle on the vinegar and lemon juice and toss lightly. Serve at once.

MANGOES IN CHAMPAGNE

Serves 6

Begin preparation of this simple but delicious dessert about 1 hour before serving time. Eliminate the Grand Marnier if preferred, and remember that you can substitute a little orange juice or concentrate topped up with soda water instead of champagne.

3 large, ripe mangoes
1 tbsp Grand Marnier or preferred orange liqueur
1 bottle brut champagne, well chilled
6 strawberries, hulled, washed and dried

Peel and slice the mangoes and place slices into champagne flutes. Sprinkle a little Grand Marnier into each glass and chill until serving time.

To serve, add a strawberry to each glass, pour on the champagne and serve immediately, with long-handled spoons. If using orange juice and soda water, add the juice before mangoes are chilled, then top up with soda at serving time.

A VERY SPECIAL DINNER FOR TWO

From time to time, special occasions are best shared by just two — birthdays, anniversaries, or whatever — and this menu is planned for just such a celebration.

The food does not involve a lot of last minute preparation, but it is delicate and subtle in its flavours.

VEGETABLE CONSOMME WITH CORN AND CHIVE MADELEINES

POACHED TURKEY FILLET WITH CHAMPAGNE

WILD RICE NESTS WITH HONEY GLAZED ROOT VEGETABLES

GREEN SALAD WITH AVOCADO SLICES*

ALMOND MERINGUES WITH STRAWBERRIES IN BALSAMIC VINEGAR

VEGETABLE CONSOMME

Serves 4

Although the quantity required for this menu is only for two, it is worth making the extra amount and freezing it for another meal. A light and delicate soup, this is a simple, classic variation on a basic consomme.

2 tbsp butter
1 baby white turnip, peeled and finely diced
2 baby carrots, peeled and finely diced
2 very small leeks (white part only), well washed and
  finely shredded
1 small stalk of celery, finely diced or sliced
little freshly ground pepper
1 tbsp tiny green peas or finely sliced snow peas
5 cups clear strong beef bouillon
2 tbsps dry sherry
freshly chopped chervil leaves or chives

In a medium saucepan, melt butter over moderate heat. Add turnip, carrot, leek and celery and stir for 1 minute. Add pepper. Reduce heat to low, cover saucepan and cook gently for another 2 minutes. Add 1 cup of the beef bouillon; cook for 15 minutes. Add remaining liquid, peas and sherry. Raise heat, bring soup to the boil, stirring once or twice, and cook for 2 minutes. Pour into heated bowls and sprinkle with chervil or chives.

Serve immediately with warm Corn and Chive Madeleines.

CORN AND CHIVE MADELEINES

Makes about 60 tiny ones or 12 large

Madeleine tins are readily available at most cookware shops nowadays (they seem to be coming into fashion here!) and their dainty shell shape looks most attractive. However, baked in a shallow patty pan tray, they will look a little less interesting, but the flavour will be just as good.

½ cup yellow cornmeal
6 tbsp plain flour
1 tsp sugar
little salt (optional)
good pinch cayenne pepper
2 tbsp butter, melted
½ cup buttermilk
1 large egg
2 tbsp chopped chives (I like to break up and add their
   flower heads as well)

Preheat oven to 200°C and butter 60 tiny tins or 12 large tins. Place dry ingredients into a food processor and mix for a few seconds.
Add the melted butter and mix for a few seconds, then add buttermilk, egg and chives. Using pulse control on the processor, 'pulse' 10 times. Stir in the flowers, if using. Spoon into the tins.

   Bake the small ones for only 6–8 minutes, the large for about 20 minutes.

They may be cooked in advance and reheated in foil at 190°C for about 8 minutes.

POACHED TURKEY FILLET WITH CHAMPAGNE

Serves 2

The lean meat of turkey is an excellent choice for healthy eating and, of course, the breast has virtually no fat at all. If preferred, a dry white wine may be substituted for the champagne. Remember that the alcohol will be removed by the cooking heat and that the other courses of this meal balance the inclusion of a little butter and cream in the main dish.

375g turkey breast fillets
1 onion, sliced
½ cup dry sherry
1 tsp fresh thyme leaves or ½ tsp dried thyme
black pepper

3 cups rich chicken stock or turkey stock
½ cup leek greens
3 spring onions, chopped
1 stalk celery with leaves, chopped
1 sprig thyme
few sprigs parsley, including stalks

1 tbsp butter
1 extra leek, washed carefully
1 stalk celery
1 carrot
½ cup watercress sprigs

1 cup dry champagne
⅓ cup cream
pepper

GARNISHES

blanched leek greens, approximately 7.5 cm long
lightly cooked carrot straws, 5 cm long
additional watercress

Prepare fillets by removing skin, gristle etc. Place into a shallow dish and add onion, sherry, thyme and black pepper. Cover dish and marinate 24 hours.

To cook dish, prepare a mirepoix by coarsely chopping the leek greens, spring onions, celery, stalk and leaves, thyme and parsley. Place into a saucepan with the stock. Allow to cook until liquid is reduced to about 1 cup. Strain through muslin, return liquid to the saucepan and continue cooking until reduced to ½ – ¾ cup.

Chop the extra leek, celery, carrot and watercress sprig. Melt butter in a heavy lidded frypan or saucepan. Place chopped vegetables into the butter and sauté very gently until vegetables have softened. Remove turkey fillet from marinade and place on vegetables. Strain marinade into reserved stock and pour the liquid over turkey fillet and vegetables. Cover saucepan or pan and cook very gently for 30–40 minutes. Turn fillet once or twice during cooking time. Test turkey with a skewer and if liquid runs clear, remove turkey, wrap in foil and keep warm in a very low oven.

Raise heat under saucepan or pan and cook until vegetables are tender. Pour in champagne and continue cooking until liquid has almost evaporated. Spoon vegetables and liquid into blender or processor and blend until mixture is quite smooth; return mixture to pan, add cream and simmer until sauce reduces and thickens.

Meanwhile, blanch leek greens and cook carrot straws.

To serve, slice turkey fillet diagonally. Spoon sauce onto 2 heated plates and arrange turkey slices on it. Garnish with leek and carrot straws, and watercress sprigs; serve with butternut balls and whole green beans.

WILD RICE NESTS WITH HONEY GLAZED ROOT VEGETABLES

Serves 2

If wild rice is a little too extravagant, even for a special occasion, use a mixture of long grain brown rice and wild rice. An even cheaper alternative is to use the Chinese black sticky rice, cooked only until it is of the texture of ordinary rice, rather than the glutinous consistency at which it is usually served.

little butter
125g wild rice
well-flavoured turkey or chicken stock
2 small carrots, julienned
1 small parsnip, julienned
1 baby Swede turnip (if available)
1 tbsp butter
1 tsp honey
little pepper and nutmeg
very, very finely chopped parsley

Melt the butter in a frying pan, add the rice and cook for about 5 minutes, stirring to prevent sticking. Bring the stock to the boil in a separate saucepan, then pour over the rice. Bring back to a simmer, cover pan tightly and reduce heat to low. Cook for about 25 minutes or until grains are tender, but not splitting.

Meanwhile, steam the vegetables which have been peeled and julienned. Add butter, honey, pepper and nutmeg to the vegetables and sauté gently, turning occasionally, until they are warmed through and coated with the glaze.

To make the nests, spoon a portion of rice onto each plate, hollow out the centre with a spoon and pile in the vegetables. Sprinkle with the fine flecks of parsley.

ALMOND MERINGUES WITH STRAWBERRIES IN BALSAMIC VINEGAR

Makes about 12 meringues

A sweet morsel to end the meal; I suggest you serve only one or two meringues each. The remainder will keep well in a tightly sealed container.

Although balsamic vinegar is suggested as an added flavour, it is optional and, of course, you may prefer to add a dash of your favourite liqueur. I find this delicious Italian style of serving berries is perfect as a contrast with the sweetness of the meringues.

MERINGUES

3 egg whites
185g granulated sugar (of course this is the naughty element!)
90 toasted blanched almonds, finely chopped
½ tsp vanilla essence
1 cup small strawberries (or preferred berries)
little whipped cream (optional)
toasted flaked almonds

Beat egg whites very stiffly, then beat in 4 tablespoons of the sugar. When mixture is glassy and well peaked, fold in the rest of the sugar, the chopped almonds and the vanilla. Mix in very, very lightly, but thoroughly.

Spoon the meringue mixture onto a lightly buttered scone tray and bake in a low oven (120°C) for 1¾–2 hours or until the meringues are fawn in colour and crisp when touched. Meanwhile, place fruit into a bowl and add about 2 teaspoons of balsamic vinegar and a touch of sugar. Allow to stand for about 30 minutes, then drain off liquid and serve the berries with the meringues.

Note: Balsamic vinegar, available from good grocery stores and specialist food shops, is a full-flavoured, cask-aged vinegar. Although it has a sharp edge to its flavour, it is rich and mellow and quite different from most vinegars we use.

CHICKEN STOCK

Throughout this book I refer frequently to homemade chicken stock, as I feel it is an essential ingredient in many dishes. Apart from their saltiness, I do not feel that cubes or powders offer the same true chicken flavour. (However, if you are pressed for time, you will no doubt occasionally be lured by the fast cube!)

This stock is the basis for a variety of soups and sauces and it is worth making up a reasonable quantity and freezing it. I find well washed milk cartons make excellent containers for freezing. It is then a simple matter to peel the paper from the frozen block of stock and to thaw it in the saucepan in which it is to be used.

Boiling hens may be used for the stock but carcasses are cheap to buy from the local 'chook shop' and are satisfactory for this purpose.

2kg chicken carcasses, including wings, necks, feet etc.
  if available
2 carrots, roughly chopped
2 onions, studded with 2 cloves, and halved
1 stalk celery with leaves, chopped
1 leek, very well washed and thickly sliced
4 parsley sprigs
1 small bay leaf
6 black peppercorns
3lt cold water

Place all ingredients into a large stockpot (and if you don't own one, it is a really worthwhile investment). Bring to the boil and skim often. Simmer gently, uncovered, for about 2 hours, skimming frequently.

Strain into a bowl and, when quite cold, cover and refrigerate overnight.

Carefully remove every scrap of fat which settles on the surface and discard. Strain stock through a chinoise or muslin. (An old, well washed nylon curtain works well.) Use as required or pour into a container, label and freeze.

RICH BEEF STOCK

This is another essential ingredient in many of our recipes, and can provide a beautiful dish in itself. I love a rich beef stock into which a couple of spring onions and a few mushrooms have been chopped – just simmer it until the vegetables are tender, add a little chopped parsley and eat as a wonderful, super-light meal.

If you have your own favourite recipe for beef stock, use it by all means. If not, you will find this is a good one. The meat doesn't have much flavour after it has been simmered for so long, but Rosie, my giant standard French poodle, regards it as a doggy gourmet's delight!

3 kg beef bones
750 g gravy beef, diced
1 tbsp unsalted butter or margarine
2 large carrots, thickly sliced
2 large onions, thickly sliced
2 stalks celery, sliced
1 well washed leek, thickly sliced (greens and all)
6 mushrooms, coarsely sliced
6 peppercorns, lightly crushed
about 4 lt cold water

Heat butter until very hot and brown the bones and meat until very well darkened. Add carrot and onion and continue to brown. Add celery, leek and all remaining ingredients, including the water. Bring to the boil, reduce to a simmer and cook, uncovered, for at least 4 hours. Remove any surface scum frequently – this helps ensure the stock will not be cloudy. Strain stock through a sieve, cool, cover and chill in refrigerator overnight.

Next morning, remove every trace of fat from the surface and discard. Strain through a chinoise or muslin into a large bowl. Use as required or pour into containers and freeze.

Note: If a denser, richer stock is needed, continue to simmer stock after second straining until it is reduced to desired consistency.

INDEX

135

— Poached pears with ginger and pistachios 107
— Raspberry bavarian mould with fresh berries 83
— Ruby poached apples with spiced wine syrup 66
— Simmered quinces 94
— Spiced koshav 77
DIPS
— Curry cream dip 117
— Smoked oyster and tuna dip 105
DRESSINGS
— Anchovy dressing 65
— Dressing 34
— French dressing 53
— Lemon mayonnaise 17
— Mustard yoghurt dressing 119

EGGS
— Pickled eggs 38
— Scotch quail eggs 96

Fig flowers with fragrant raspberries 45
Figs poached in red wine with orange segments 18
FISH
— Crispy tuna rolls 52
— Grilled trout 114
Flambéed fruits with shredded crêpes 10
French dressing 53
Fresh fig and walnut cake 85
Fresh fig and watercress salad 20
Fresh fruit salad 115
Fruit flambé 10

Garlic and lemon marinated chicken kebabs 7
Golden soup with brown rice 49
Gourmet potatoes 111
Gratinée of summer fruits 28
Grilled trout 114

Herbed mushroom pâté 51
Herbed olives 73
Homemade liptauer cheese 50
Homemade muesli 12
Homemade pita bread 75

Italian tomato salad 65

Kofta skewers with basil buttered pita bread 74

Latticed butternut tartlets in sunflower seed crust 69
Leanne's sponge 88
Lebanese salad 105
Lemon mayonnaise 17
Lemon peel shreds 112
Lemon tea loaf 90
Lemon water ice 112
Liberty house blueberry muffins 13
Liptauer cheese, homemade 50

Madeleines, corn and chive 128
Mangoes in champagne 125
Mango and toasted pecan ice cream 71
MEATS
— Braised veal shanks with gremolada 63
— Kofta skewers with basil buttered pita bread 74
— Middle Eastern meatballs with coriander flavoured sauce 106
— Rosemary racks of lamb 110
Medley of summer garden delights 8
Medley of wild and brown rices with mushrooms of field and forest 81
Middle Eastern meatballs with coriander flavoured sauce 106
Minted brown rice salad 53
Muesli, homemade 12
Muffins, blueberry 13
Mushroom and mixed green salad 27
Mustard coated spatchcock 26
Mustard yoghurt dressing 119

Naughty but nice chocolate mousse 99

Olives, herbed 73